LIVE SUNNY SIDE UP!

THE B'S OF JOYFUL LIVING: DISCOVER LIFE'S JOY AND PURPOSE

WRITTEN BY AURORA A. AMBROSE

DEDICATION

To the love of my life, my parents, family and friends, with utmost gratitude for your loving encouragement; Also, to those who have shed light, wisdom and help when I needed it most. Thank you so much for your loving care, prayers, patience, time, support and inspiration.

MY PURPOSE

O God, Thou art my God; early will I seek Thee: my soul thirsteth for Thee, my flesh longeth for Thee in a dry and thirsty land, where no water is; To see Thy power and Thy glory, so as I have seen Thee in the sanctuary. Because Thy loving kindness is better than life, my lips shall praise Thee. Thus will I bless Thee while I live: I wil lift up my hands in Thy Name. My soul shall be satisfied as with marrow and fatness; and my mouth shall praise Thee with joyful lips: when I remember Thee upon my bed, and meditate on Thee in the night watches. Because Thou hast been my help, therefore in the shadow of Thy wings will I rejoice. My soul followeth hard after Thee: Thy right hand upholdeth me. - Psalm 63:1-8 KJV

All Bible Scriptures are referenced from either the King James Version or the New International Versions, unless otherwise noted.

TABLE OF CONTENTS

Prologue

Be Filled With Inexpressible Joy!

When you look around you, what brings you joy? How often do you feel and express joy? The word Joy is so important to our lives that this word is mentioned 162 times in the Holy Bible. There is so much joy to glean, appreciate and share each day of our lives! Actually, the moment we awaken each day, among the very first thoughts in our minds should be those of joyful glee and deep appreciation for being alive another day. Nothing we have done has earned us this gift of being alive, yet God deems us so valuable to Himself that He awakens us to see another blessed day.

What a truly marvelous gift! One reason that I am full of joy is because of the hope, love and faith I have in Jesus. The joy of the Lord is my Strength, for He turns my darkest days and most trying difficulties into more meaningful and beautiful experiences. Life is full of situations, people and challenges that would steal your joy if you allowed them to. Yet I realize that it is up to me to choose the things, people and situations that endow me and others with more strength, joy and realize more poignantly the manifestations of the best I am designed to be.

It is not about me, but it is about the opportunity to be. The power to choose is mine, and it is also yours. What do you choose to be? What do you choose to do, with this gift of life? What do you choose to become? Are you using your power to choose wisely for the greater good? He makes every day in my life a joyful experience as He brings out the best in me, no matter how life may try to steal my joy. Another reason to rejoice is to celebrate the joy of Jesus Christ's birth, the real reason for the Christmas season and for the inexpressible joy we can have every day of the year! Since my childhood, I was taught that faith, perseverance, diligence, discipline, courage, patience, inspiration, hope and joy enable a person to endure, grow and thrive. Since my childhood, I sang and read hymns and Christmas carols, for the inspirational words of the songs, like the words of the Bible, speak to my heart. Truly, we are blessed beyond description, so let us rejoice daily!

JOY TO THE WORLD

The lyrics of the popular Christmas carol, entitled "Joy to the World," were written in 1719 by Isaac Watts who lived from 1674-1748. Watts was ordained as a Pastor of an Independent congregation. Isaac Watts wrote many hymns and carols. He was awarded a Doctor of Divinity degree by the University of Edinburgh in 1728. The music to this carol is by George Frederick Handel, who lived from 1685-1759.

 "Joy to the World" is based on Psalm 98 in the Bible, which is noted as one of the Royal Psalms, particularly Psalms 93-99. These passages of scripture praise God as the King of His people. Portions of Psalm 98 inspired me to write this book: 1) "Sing to the Lord a new song, for He has done marvelous things…3) He has remembered His love and His faithfulness (When I think of all of His love, mercy, grace and faithfulness to me all the years of my life, I am filled with inexpressible joy!)…4) Shout for joy to the Lord, all the earth, burst into jubilant song with music." Let us realize that we have so much to be grateful for! Take a moment to slow down from life's hectic pace. Look around you and notice the beauty of Joy. Joy does not only live in the major moments of life. True Joy lives in all the little things that make life meaningful. As you read this book, "Live Sunny Side Up," learn how you can live more joyfully. Get ready to find the Joy you have been looking for!

Joy to the world, the Lord is come! Let earth receive her King;

Let every heart prepare Him room, and Heaven and nature sing,

And Heaven and nature sing, and Heaven, and Heaven, and nature sing.

Joy to the world, the Savior reigns! Let men their songs employ;

While fields and floods, rocks, hills and plains repeat the sounding joy, repeat the sounding joy, repeat, repeat, the sounding joy.

No more let sins and sorrows grow, Nor thorns infest the ground;

He comes to make His blessings flow far as the curse is found,

Far as the curse is found, far as, far as, the curse is found.

He rules the world with truth and grace and makes the nations prove the glories of His righteousness and wonders of His love,

And wonders of His love.

And wonders, wonders, of His love.

The words, "Wonders of His Love" speak to my heart for God's endless love is enveloping like a tender embrace. His love, totally undeserved, is so warm and giving that we are never without it even in our darkest hours. Bask in His love, receive it and embrace it. Open your heart to Him and God will bless you.

"Drinking from My Saucer:" Anonymous

I've never made a fortune and it's probably too late now, but I don't worry about that much 'cause I'm happy anyhow. As I go along life's way, I'm reaping better than I sowed. I'm drinking from my saucer 'cause my cup has overflowed. Haven't got a lot of riches and sometimes the going's tough, But I've got loving ones around me and that makes me rich enough. I thank God for His blessings and the mercies He's bestowed. I'm drinking from my saucer 'cause my cup has overflowed. Oh, I remember times when everything all went wrong. My faith wore somewhat thin, but all at once, the dark clouds broke and the sun peeped through again. So Lord, please help me not to gripe about the many tough rows I've hoed. I am drinking from my saucer 'cause my cup has overflowed. If God gives me strength and courage when the way grows steep and rough, I'll not ask for other blessings 'cause I'm already blessed enough. May I never be too busy to help others bear their loads, for I'll be drinking from my saucer 'cause my cup has overflowed.

INTRODUCTION

BE WISER, RISE HIGHER: CHOOSE YOUR ATTITUDE AND ALTITUDE

Truly, one's attitude determines one's altitude in life's journey. That attitude or perspective colors everything in life. In my opinion, the more positive one's attitude is, the higher their altitude will be. Therefore, your perspective is your elective. That said, living sunny side up, like a fresh daisy, upturned towards the sun, is my lifestyle, by choice. It is said that I tend to have a sunny disposition. That means that being intentionally cheerful, optimistic, upbeat, cooperative, encouraging and motivated, with a ready smile on my face and a song in my heart, is my usual choice of mindset. That is correct. I said, it is my choice of mindset. The same can be true for you if that is your decision. In this age where one's brand is one's life or business, did you ever think about what your brand is? Oh, you don't need to have a business to have a brand, for your brand is everything you are, say, do and believe. It is what you show day in and day out. What do people know about you? Are you upbeat and productive, or always finding fault with something or someone? Are you accepting of your responsibility for where you are in life, or are you blaming everyone else for your plight? As it is often said, "every tub has to stand on its own four feet," so let us choose to brand ourselves and our lives with the joie de vie, or joy of life, and the attitude of gratitude, we all were designed for.

Since our greatest power is to choose, we must set our minds daily, by expressing gratitude to God upon awakening as we count our blessings; by praying, listening to the wisdom He imparts; by reading a portion of scripture in order to properly guide our steps during the day; and by choosing to take one moment at a time, inspired to solve problems, rather than letting problems drown us in a multitude of "Oh, woe is me, life is so bad" pity parties. Therefore, having an attitude of gratitude is fundamental to the joy that keeps me buoyant. True joy is not based on the circumstances of the day, for circumstances can be misleading. I've seen people who appear, on the surface, to have the most enviable life: the best career, expensive material possessions and fame, yet I have witnessed their expressed laments about the emptiness they found awaiting them at the zenith of their climb to the top. Instead, joy is a direct result of living in God's presence. I know this because He is my Anchor. He keeps me afloat in the ocean of life. Yes, difficulties come and they go. When I stay in daily, active communication with the Lord, some problems resolve themselves and others I learn to deal with to get them resolved. Through it all, God is with me, assisting me with situations as I remain close to Him. He is my lifeline, my life jacket and as such, His joy is my strength, enabling me to have a sunny disposition. I often reflect on the following passages from the Bible, my GPS, which I reference often in my writing from either the King James Version or the New International Version, so those scriptures are usually noted as Book Name 3:17-19. For example, here are two of my favorite passages, the first noted in Habakkuk, chapter 3, verses 17-19, and the second is from Psalm 63:1-8. Both are certainly applicable to this discussion, as they express my purpose. May they also express yours. *"Though the fig tree does not bud and there are no grapes on the vines, though the olive crop fails and the fields produce no food, though there are no sheep in the pen and no cattle in the stalls, Yet I will rejoice in the Lord, I will be joyful in God my Savior. The Soverign Lord is my strength; He makes my feet like the feet of a deer, He enables me to go on the heights."* NIV

O God, Thou art my God; early will I seek Thee: my soul thirsteth for Thee, my flesh longeth for Thee in a dry and thirsty land, where no water is; To see Thy power and Thy glory, so as I have seen Thee in the sanctuary. Because Thy loving kindness is better than life, my lips

*shall praise Thee. Thus will I bless Thee while I live: I wil lift up my hands in Thy Name. My soul shall be satisfied as with marrow and fatness; **and my mouth shall praise Thee with joyful lips**: when I remember Thee upon my bed, and meditate on Thee in the night watches. Because Thou hast been my help, therefore in the shadow of Thy wings will I rejoice. My soul followeth hard after Thee: Thy right hand upholdeth me.* Psalm **63:1-8 KJV**

No matter what curve balls life throws at me, I will rejoice in the Lord, for He is my Savior, my deliverer, my defense, my refuge, my help and advocate Who prays for me. This knowledge and reality is just as vital to me as having my GPS, also known as the Global Positioning System, when I am traveling, in order to take the best route to my destination, for this is a common practice. You see, our attitude determines our altitude, and impacts those who we encounter during the day. As we stay prayed up and praised up with the Lord, our attitude rises higher. Sure, tough times may come our way just like they do in everyone else's life. The main difference is our focus must be on God. As for my life, He saved me, gave me a great leg up on life, so with Him, every day can be the best day ever if I will continue to trust in Him, rely on Him and let my light shine for Him as I go about my day. He can do the same for you. This is what living sunny side up means, for as we turn our faces to look upon His loving gaze, we are uplifted and enabled to keep on moving forward in our lives.

Therefore, let us choose to be *sunny side up* every day, rather than allowing ourselves to become a grouchy sourpuss, as many tend to be these days. The goal each day is to not let anything or anyone steal our joy. We are designed to overcome daily circumstances, not let circumstances overcome us. Get up, dust off and keep moving forward! So what if a bad driver cut in front of you unexpectedly. Rejoice that you are still alive and safe. Why? God has brought us all through so much that we should decide to be of good cheer! The more we rest in God's Presence, the more freely His blessings flow into us. He transforms us into a new creation in His Love. That is what love does for you. When you love someone, and someone loves you, life has a sweeter atmosphere because you know that special someone has you covered, or as I've heard it often said, "He got your back." So we can rest and be joyful on that strong foundation. Although life in this world is full of difficulties, problems and trials, which are designed to develop patience and fortitude, our faith in Christ keeps us believers strong, encouraged and ever moving forward, knowing that God's got our back, sides, front, in fact, He has us covered from head to toe. So there is no need to sweat or fret.

We all need to recognize that Life is an opportunity. Each day that we are gifted with should be treated with the utmost gratitude. We should awaken with the attitude, as I daily taught my students before retiring from 30 years of diligent service, that "I am going to make this the best day ever" by changing my attitude. No matter what happened before they walked into the classroom, we spoke our affirmations upon entering. This gave the students' day a clean start, and enabled them to ready their minds to delve into lessons without the heavy clouds of whatever was previously troubling them. They were able to concentrate without the weight of all that bearing them down. Where help was possible to address their specific needs, each one was addressed by the appropriate resources that were available. My students thanked me for caring and being there consistently for them, and helping them to see a better way to view life.

Personally, this sunny attitude comes from living a life of worship, which includes prayer, Bible study, as well as time to be still and commune with God. Living sunny side up is a result of choices, determinations, revelations, transformations and inspirations, which will be shared in this book. Because of what shaped my life, some of those fundamental elements are shared herein. So many have asked me for a word of encouragement over the years. Therefore, this book is my personal prescription for my own life. It is also meant to be a source of encouragement and enlightenment to others. By no means is this a mandate for anyone else's life. However, if you see something that is of help to you, you are more than welcome to learn from it and apply it to your own life, if you choose to do so. That choice, as well as the opportunity, is all yours. If this book speaks to your heart, please tell others about it. May the lessons I have learned, expressed as **The B's of Joyful Living**, enable you to live a more fruitful, exciting life of divine favor.

The B's of Joyful Living: Be Optimistic

Let us take heed of the creed that formed my determination many years ago when I was an active member of 5-4 Optimist Club of Southern California, which inspired others to develop optimism as a philosophy of life, instill the value of volunteering in today's youth, develop citizens who have respect for the law, respect for themselves, and respect for the improvement of all communities:

The Optimist Creed: Promise Yourself

To be so strong that nothing can disturb your peace of mind. To talk health, happiness and prosperity to every person you meet. To make all your friends feel that there is something special in them. To look at the sunny side of everything and make your optimism come true. To think only of the best, to work only for the best, and to expect only the best. To be just as enthusiastic about the success of others as you are about your own. To forget the mistakes of the past and press on to the greater achievements of the future. To wear a cheerful countenance at all times and give every living creature you meet a smile. To give so much time to the improvement of yourself that you have no time to criticize others. To be too large for worry, too noble for anger, too strong for fear, and too happy to permit the presence of trouble.

Enough said, for the creed is self explanatory. Do you know where the phrase "sunny side " comes from? Well, according to WikiPedia, it was in 1899 that Ada Blenkhorn was inspired to write a Christian hymn, coined by a phrase that her young nephew often used. Blenkhorn's nephew was disabled. When being taken for a stroll outside, he always wanted his wheelchair pushed down "the sunny side" of the street. Once the Carter Family heard of the song from A. P. Carter's uncle, who was a music teacher, they recorded that song in Camden, New Jersey in 1928. "Keep on the Sunny Side" became their theme song on the radio in later years. Since words frame our lives with substance and meaning, may these lyrics, upon which the theme of this book is based, encourage and uplift you:

There's a dark and a troubled side of life; There's a bright and a sunny side, too; Tho' we meet with the darkness and strife, The sunny side we also may view. Keep on the sunny side, always on the sunny side, Keep on the sunny side of life; It will help us every day, it will brighten all the way,If we keep on the sunny side of life. Tho' the storm in its fury break today, Crushing hopes that we cherished so dear, Storm and cloud will in time pass away, The sun again will shine bright and clear. **Let us greet with a song of hope each day, Tho' the moments be cloudy or fair; Let us trust in our Savior alway, Who keepeth everyone in His care.**

What does this song mean by the words "keep on the sunny side?" Here in the last four lines, noted in bold letters, the phrase means to anticipate each new day with a hopeful perspective, and live each day with faith and trust in God. The sunny side is determined by the words we say, the thoughts we think and our choice of actions. They are all related. As we think, so we are. Choose to be upbeat and positive, then watch the change in your mood, temperament and health.

Did you know that there is power in our words and thoughts? Yes, indeed. Whatever we say, we cause to happen by the energy we give it through the spoken word. What we choose, so it will be. Choose to speak life, joy, health and strength instead of speaking what is dark, dreary, anxious, full of complaints and negative. It is just that simple, yet that complex. Notice what is written in Philippians 4:4-7: [4] *Rejoice in the Lord always. I will say it again: Rejoice!* [5] *Let your gentleness be evident to all. The Lord is near.* [6] *Do not be anxious about anything, but in every situation, by prayer and petition, with thanksgiving, present your requests to God.* [7] *And the peace of God, which transcends all understanding, will guard your hearts and your minds in Christ Jesus.* This explains that unmitigated, incontainable joy should distinctively mark every believer in Jesus Christ. After all, as stated previously, Christian joy is not based on one's circumstances nor on religion. It is based on one's relationship with the Lord and the deep, abiding spiritual quality of life that comes from fellowship with Him, realizing how truly blessed one is. So rejoicing in the Lord is the key, no matter what may be, for He is with you, providing the grace, joy and strength to keep on keeping on.

I am reminded of the optimistic determination and dedication of the world's oldest female bodybuilder, Ernestine Shepherd. After listening to her interviews on YouTube, and with Dr. Mehmet Oz, I was shocked to learn that this vibrant, young lady I observed was actually 78 years of age! With the fitness and appearance of someone 50 years her junior, she related her love for people and her gratitude for her many blessings as she shared her motivation and strategies for achieving this Guinness Book of World Records accomplishment. In her interview, she encouraged and enlightened listeners with the following:

"My sister, Velvet, and I went shopping for bathing suits. When we saw how we looked in the mirror, we decided to do something about it. I was such a prissy woman. I didn't want to do any of that exercising. My sister was very active. When she started working out, she was 99 pounds and skin and bones. She had to gain enough weight to meet her goal of 140 pounds, which she did. I was 145 pounds so I had to come down in weight because I had all the cellulite, I had the fat in the back, and my legs were…Oh, my God… they were a mess. We were complete opposites.

I made a promise to my sister that I would follow her dream, and it has become mine. She said that we wanted to inspire and motivate others to live a healthy, happy and fit lifestyle, to let them know that age is nothing but a number, and you can get fit. After my sister died from a brain aneurysm, I ended up with high blood pressure, panic attacks, high cholesterol, you name it, I had it. After a lot of prayer and help from my family, I could get on my feet again, and I started running. I found out I didn't need to take all that medication I was taking. My blood pressure went down, I stopped feeling unhappy, I stopped feeling depressed. People I know and people I don't know inspire me to keep going. They tell me how I'm helping them, and that was what my sister's and my dream was. So as long as I have breath in my body, that's what I want to do.

When my sister and I began working out, she said, "We are going to be two of the oldest competitive bodybuilders." She said we were going to make the Guinness Book of World Records by the end as two sisters. Before she died she looked at me and said, "If I don't make it, you have to continue what we started. You have to make the Guinness Book of World Records, and you have to become a bodybuilder." I met the former Mr. Universe, Yohnnie Shambourger, and I asked him if he would work with me because I wanted to become a bodybuilder. I was 71 years of age when we started. He said, "You are going on a long journey, and you are going to have to follow everything I tell you to do. Do you think you can do it?" I shook my head and said yes. In a matter of seven months, he had me ready to be on the stage. We haven't looked back since then. Many times, people ask me what I do to stay healthy. This is my daily routine and what keeps me motivated to stay in shape."

2:30 a.m. Wake up. Meditate and read devotions from the Bible. Eat a snack of a bagel with peanut butter and hard-boiled egg whites. Drink 16 oz. of water.

3:45 a.m. Head to nearby park and run 10 miles. Go home and eat breakfast of oatmeal, three hard-boiled egg whites and a tablespoon of walnuts. Drink 8 oz. of liquid egg whites.

4

8 a.m. Head to the gym and work out for 1 hour and 45 minutes.

10 to 11 a.m.: Train a group of senior men and women. The oldest woman is 89 years old.

11 a.m.: Train four to five women in the gym. Drink another 8-oz. glass of liquid egg whites.

1 p.m.: Go home and eat a can of tuna, a cup of spinach, ½ cup of sweet potato and drink an 8-oz. glass of water. REST.

6 to 7 p.m.: Teach another class at the gym. Head home and eat turkey, brown rice, broccoli, more egg whites and drink lots of water.

10 to 10:30 p.m.: Drink one more glass of liquid egg whites. Go to bed.

Now, despite all that Ernestine went through, this is proof positive that choosing to be joyfully optimistic and proactively getting into a better frame of mind can make an emphatic difference, not only in one's personal life, but also in the lives of those one encounters.

There is no need to be anxious, for that is counter productive not only to one's life but also to one's health. Often I hear people speaking only of the negatives in their lives. Listening to people during the typical day, I hear a litany of whining. Sometimes, I want to say to these people, "Get some cheese to go with your whine" but I'm sure they would not understand my message. If you dare to ask them how they are doing, usually a long laundry list of complaints comes pouring out, weighing you down the longer you listen. The more you try to encourage them, the more they complain about their situation, never once asking or caring about what is going on in your life. Instead, counting their blessings and proactively doing what can be done, getting the professional help that is needed to solve their expressed problems, is far more beneficial. For by faith, I believe that God is working on our behalf. So I refuse to be the enemy's prey, as I pray, speak, take positive action and keep on believing. All things are possible with God. This is how I stay on the sunny side.

THE BENEFITS OF STAYING ON THE SUNNY SIDE

Earlier I mentioned that the sunny side lifestyle affects our health positively. In a ten year Denmark study, researchers found that joyful, contented and enthusiastic people had a far lower occurrence of heart disease than those who felt happy less often. Also, when you shift from an anxious, hostile or depressed disposition to a sunny perspective, you fortify your immune system. In turn, this helps you avoid getting sick and even when you do get sick, you will have fewer symptoms. So a positive outlook truly makes a powerful difference in your health!

Perhaps you remember the uplifting Bobby McFerrin song, <u>Don't Worry, Be Happy</u>:

"Here's a little song I wrote; You might want to sing it note for note. Don't worry be happy. In every life we have some trouble; When you worry you make it double. Don't worry, be happy."

That popular title, "Don't Worry, Be Happy" is not just a catchy phrase. Did you know that a positive attitude can be a lifesaver, according to a recent study? In this study, researchers used a questionnaire to check the moods of 600 heart disease patients in a Denmark hospital, with a follow up five years later. They discovered that people with a positive attitude were 42 percent less likely to die during the study than those with a grumpier disposition. Also, those who were upbeat or exercised regularly were less likely to be hospitalized for a heart problem.

So no matter what comes during the day, good or bad, maintain positivity by doing the following:

- ❖ Eat good mood foods and eat at regular intervals throughout the day. By staying nutritionally fit, you keep your blood sugar stable, prevent anxiety and prevent mood swings.

❖ Get up, get moving! The more you exercise, the higher you boost your mood and protect your heart. Just twenty minutes a day combats the blues for twelve hours. Even if you sit at a desk most of the day, get up and walk at your breaks as I have done. Walking clears the mind and makes one feel energized.

This study is not the first to point out the link between being happy and being healthy. Researchers and doctors alike have long noted the direct correlation between emotional health and its effects on longevity. For example, people who are regularly pessimistic tend to suffer more chronic aches, fatigue and illness. In fact, negative emotions, like anger and sadness, also have a direct effect on brain function, increasing stress and our risk for heart disease, cancer and other serious diseases.

Proverbs 15:23. *You have joy by the answer of your mouth. So be careful what you say.*

Look on the Sunny Side

By Helen Steiner Rice

There are always two sides, the good and the bad,

The dark and the light, the sad and the glad--

But in looking back over the good and the bad

We're aware of the number of good things we've had--

And in counting our blessings we find when we're through

We've no reason at all to complain or be blue--

So thank God for good things He has already done,

And be grateful to Him for the battles you've won,

And know that the same God who helped you before

Is ready and willing to help you once more--

Then with faith in your heart reach out for God's Hand

And accept what He sends, though you can't understand--

For our Father in heaven always knows what is best,

And if you trust in His wisdom your life will be blest,

For always remember that whatever betide you,

You are never alone for God is beside you.

The Lord is my shepherd; I shall not want

He maketh me to lie down in green pastures:

He leadeth me beside the still waters.

He restoreth my soul:

He leadeth me in the paths of righteousness

for his name sake.

Yea, though I walk through the valley of the shadow of death,

I will fear no evil: for Thou art with me;

Thy rod and Thy staff they comfort me.

Thou preparest a table before me

in the presence of mine enemies:

Thou anointest my head with oil;

my cup runneth over.

Surely goodness and mercy shall follow me

all the days of my life:

and I will dwell in the house of the Lord for ever.

Psalm 23

The B's of Joyful Living

We live in a world that is far too lacking in joy due to an overabundance of attitudes and lifestyles that bring people down, rather than lift them up. Here are some suggestions for restoring joy to someone's daily life.

BE JUST LIKE AN OYSTER.

Have you ever noticed how absolutely lovely a pearl is? This uniquely natural beauty is formed by a truly miraculous process that is completely unlike the mining process that is necessary for precious metals or gemstones which are both mined from the earth. In the development of a gemstone, it must be cut and polished to bring out its full beauty. Conversely, pearls do not require this type of a treatment. In order to reveal their loveliness, a pearl must be born completely from an oyster. Its iridescence, shimmering, soft and lustrous possesses a delightful inner glow that is unlike any other gem found on earth. Please be patient with me while I further explain the reasons I am suggesting that we all be just like an oyster.

Did you know that a natural pearl begins its life as a foreign object inside an oyster? Truly it does. A foreign object, like a piece of shell or a parasite accidentally lodges itself within the oyster's soft inner body, deep down inside where it cannot be expelled. Imagine something foreign and disagreeable getting inside your throat. Perhaps this has happened to you just as it happened to me. Actually, I remember a time or two when something went down my throat incorrectly and it was stuck there. I remember swallowing repeatedly on one occasion and it went down; on another occasion, coughing brought it out and I saw a tiny piece of food come out. Have you ever eaten something that disagreed with you? Well, I did and a process began inside me that provoked vomiting the remnants out of my mouth. Gross, but it helped me begin the process of feeling better. That said, imagine the oyster, doing what it does in the ocean, just minding its business. Along comes this object that enters the oyster while it is open, just planting itself there to make a home for itself. Just like something stuck in my throat or something unpleasant in my stomach, this foreign object does not feel good. In fact, it is creating an irritating disturbance inside the oyster. To ease this unpleasant irritant, the oyster's body, just like your body and even mine, starts to take defensive action. In fact, the oyster starts to protect itself by secreting a smooth, hard crystalline substance called a nacre all around that pesky irritant. That crystalline nacre is composed of microscopic crystals of calcium carbonate, each perfectly aligned with each other, in order that the light passing along the axis of one crystal is refracted and reflected by another, producing a glorious rainbow of color and light.

While this foreign irritant stays inside the oyster's body, the oyster will busily continue to secrete more layers of crystalline nacre coatings, layer upon layer upon layer. That irritant over a period of time will be totally encased by multiple layers of silkiness, created by the hard, smooth crystalline coatings, resulting in this uniquely gorgeous pearl. What an amazing wonder is this miraculous process where one of nature's most beautiful surprises is created just from the oyster protecting itself! Of course, there is a difference between natural and cultured pearls. Oysters will form a cultured pearl in the same way that a natural pearl is formed. However, instead of leaving the process to a chance occurrence, the difference is that a person will carefully implant an irritant inside the oyster, stepping back to let nature create its amazing miracle of lustrous beauty.

Just thinking about this process demonstrates how we are to be in our daily lives. There is a popular, anonymous adage that every day may not be good, but there is something good in every day. Romans 12:21 says do not be overcome by evil, but overcome evil with good. Certainly, just as I have, we all may have encountered someone in our personal or professional lives who seems stuck in negativity, as evidences by their daily comments, attitude and behavior. Unbeknownst to him or her, this person is an energy vampire, draining you of your optimism and joy if defensive action is not taken.

Like the oyster, you need to know how to deal with this for this person has been planted in your circle of influence. I have worked with people who are incessantly negative. I was working with one person who talked nonsense and negativity the entire time we were on the same assignment. Every time this person said something negative, I countered with something positive and proceeded to continue my theme until the person suddenly left. I breathed a sigh of relief and continued to listen on my ear buds to the spiritual nourishment that strengthens and sustains me. God's Word, traditional and contemporary gospel music, faith stories, inspirational podcasts, biographies of those who made it despite tough odds and good, clean humor are all instruments of rebuilding my faith and fortitude. For what is poured out of me, must be refilled in order for me to continue to be who I am designed to be.

Now this person was a tough assignment, for sure, but all believers are called to positively influence the world around us. It is our assignment to be a witness for Jesus Christ and be a positive reservoir of His light and love. Positive people, because of Christ being their center, have overcome their fears to such a degree that their beautiful energy flows outwardly. Consequently, they give energy instead of taking it, for in their presence, because of Who Christ is to them, you tend to feel energized, inspired, uplifted and ready to take on life's challenges rather than succumb to them. However, the Bible tells clearly tells us not to be overcome by evil, but we are to overcome evil with good. Sure, you may prefer to just exit stage left but what good is light if it will not change the darkness around it? What good is salt if it will not change the flavor of the food it placed upon? So, we know that this type of person has an endless capacity to dwell only on everything negative. Every time you see this person, they tend to complain, whine and moan about their lives, refusing to take responsibility for the results they see in their own lives. This person is full of fear, which blocks the natural flow of everything positive that is within him or her. Since they are choosing (yes, this is their conscious choice) to block their own positivity or inner light from God, they must get that light and positivity from others. Realize that just because a negative person has an endless supply of pity party invitations, "oh, woe is me," you do not have to choose to RSVP.

L O V E
bears all things,
believes all things,
hopes all things,
endures all things.
- 1 Cor. 13:7

Reach Out

So, as oysters, let us consider how we can help a mildly or temporarily negative person who is drowning in a negative mindset. First of all, overcome darkness with light. Reach out with a kind word or gesture to cheer him or her up. Keep the conversation positive. Take him or her out to eat and talk about positive memories together. Sometimes just some positive attention is all that is needed to turn things around.

Throw Out

If this method is not successful, throw out the life line or the life preserver. Perhaps this person is much further out in the ocean of negativity. Maybe he or she is in denial of their problem even though everyone else can see it clearly. So, consider throwing out a life line or life preserver through a more indirect approach to help bolster their spirit. Give them a card or letter to show how much you care, or tell the person how much you care during a conversation. Use humor to break up the negative train of thought and bring him or her back to the shore of balance. One example of helping this type of person is to use an upbeat audio message or photo to insert into their electronic device. Send an inspirational message, YouTube video or song, as I have often done. I have even sent myself a song, link, photo or message, for it re-energizes me during my busy day. You see, everyone can benefit from a positive message.

It is just like when I was watching the television program, The Best of the Joy of Painting, where Bob Ross is demonstrating stroke by stroke how to paint lovely images. I watched one day as he painted a farmhouse scene, using dark hues to offset the lighter ones, creating a lovely softening effect much like an impressionist painter uses to develop the completed work. In the same way, the words we speak and the actions we choose can soften and sweeten the lives around us. After all, I have had my tough moments in life, and I am so grateful that someone chose to come alongside me each time and lend me a helping hand.

Row Out

Another great method to help a negative person is to row out to them with an intervention. Get several positive people together and visit the negative person. This gives more leverage than going alone would do, particularly if alcohol or drug influence is a factor in either the cause or the continuity of the negativity. Cast the light of awareness on what this person's words and actions are doing to worsen their situation. Offer all the combined help and resources that you can bring to the table. Help this person find their way out of the tunnel of darkness into the light. Extending the rowboat of hope, for there is always hope no matter how dark or foreboding things may appear to be. There is hopeful intervention in many organizations that help people through the roughest of situations: shelters like The Sheepfold for those who have been abused or endangered in some way, local churches that offer teaching and resources to mitigate difficult situations, ministries that help the homeless, organizations like food banks that feed the hungry and many more resources to help with every difficulty that people experience. Whatever is needed, seek out the help on the negative person's behalf. We are so fortunate to live in a world filled with free information right at our fingertips. Google, Bing, Ask.com and several other Internet search engines are available to research what is needed and render assistance in a timely manner, by pointing the way to where best that help can be found.

Go Out

As a last resort of assistance to someone who is struggling with negativity, try working one on one with the person to lift them up and bear them out of the incessantly negative mindset. However, just as in helping someone who is drowning, one must be careful remain positive so as not to be inundated and sucked down into their negative energy. Remember to keep yourself safe at all times with a gentle combination of genuine caring and detached awareness. You are the lifeguard. Do not allow yourself to be drowned by feeling so sorry for the person's sad story that you lose perspective on your purpose for being there. Stay positive, encouraging and upbeat. Above all, pray this person through their struggles. By seeking Divine help from the Lord, the Maker of heaven and earth, faith in His ability to turn things around for the best good can help, in addition to faith focused audio and written resources. All of these can enable one to choose love over fear, as we let go and let God help us overcome the most difficult of situations. One way that I help people is to quote song lyrics or a poem to uplift their spirits. One of my favorite songs that speaks to many hearts is written by Marvin Winans, who wrote:

"I've had some good days. I've had some hills to climb. I've had some weary days. I've had some sleepless nights but when I look around and I think things over, all of my good days outweigh my bad days, so I won't complain. Sometimes the clouds hang low. I can hardly see the road and then I ask the question, 'Lord, why so much pain?' But He knows what's best for me, although my weary eyes can't see, so I'll just say, 'Thank You Lord, I won't complain. God's been so good to me. The Lord has been so good to me, more than this old world or you could ever be. The Lord has been so good to me and He dried my tears away and He turned all my midnights into days. So I'll say, 'Thank You Lord. 'Thank You Lord. 'Thank You Lord.' I won't complain."

BE JOYFUL

Certainly, it is not always easy to be joyful at all times in our lives. Still, with the right perspective and a grateful heart, we can try to change our attitude. Although loneliness, sorrow, suffering and pain are a part of life, we can choose to look up and thank God for the lives we live, or we can choose to become bitter and focused on the suffering, forgetting that life on earth is only for a second, but eternity and where we spend it is forever. The second fruit of the Holy Spirit is joy, a concept which is further explained in the next chapter, entitled "Be Fruitful." Speaking to His disciples, Christ said in John 15:11, *"These things have I spoken unto you, that My joy might remain in you, and that your joy might be full."* In the Greek language, this word "joy" is translated as chara, which means cheerfulness, calm delight, and gladness.

Healthier and Happier for the First Time Ever

Having a joyful outlook is helping me achieve my lifelong dreams and inspire others to do the same. At work, in my daily activities and at the parks where I often exercise reflectively, there is such a joyful connection with others who share their stories with me as we encourage each other along the way. Since my thyroidectomy and goiter removal surgery, I gained back much of the weight I had just worked so hard to lose prior to my operation, recovery, due to the inability to move fluidly during recovery, attacked by constant excruciating pain. My head had to be kept upright in order for the stitches to heal properly. Talking was not allowed. Even the usual body movements had to be restricted, and every movement caused a deeper aching, which was helped greatly by the pain medication. Yet I remained grateful, so thankful to be alive and able to function more and more as each day of the four month recovery period passed. Although homebound, in the lovely stillness, I read and listened to encouragement, observed nature and wildlife, listened to hymns, gospel music and upbeat messages, many of which brought tears of abundant gratitude to my eyes. I particularly enjoy Bill and Gloria Gaither's program, "Precious Memories," full of inspirational songs and shared life stories. So many cards, calls and letters spoke to my heart! Eventually, I was able to type on my laptop to stay in touch with friends and loved ones. Time seemed to move at a snail's pace, yet I rejoiced to be visited by dear friends and feel God's abiding loving care through those He planted around me, enabling me to bloom in appreciation, wisdom, and courage. As more time passed, I was given the green light to talk and move about more, yet driving was still impossible since I could not turn my neck fully without turning my whole body. You never realize just how much your functioning depends on the mobility of your neck until something like this happens. Oh, how grateful I am to be able to move my whole body now! Now I stretch like a cat before moving, turn on music to do a little dance, occasionally I skip instead of walk, and when I see a swing, I'm on it like white on rice, swinging and kicking my legs gleefully!

Upon returning to the parks, I was welcomed heartily by the lovely wildlife and fellow exercisers. I felt God's Presence all around me, cheering me on, step by step. I thoroughly enjoy breathing in and out the fresh, fragrant, unpolluted air and seeing so many fraternizing geese, pigeons, sparrows, finches, swans and a wide assortment of ducks along my path, as I recalled the words of the hymn, "Why should I feel discouraged, why should the shadows fall? Why should my heart be lonely and long for heaven and home, when Jesus is my portion. My constant friend is He. His eye is on the sparrow, and I know He watches me." Overall, this helped me get my drive back. I'm feeling stronger, able to walk three miles around the perimeter of the park. Sometimes I sing, although only for a short period of time as that becomes painful with increased duration. Yet this joy I have is uncontainable, inspiring me to push forward and motivate others to be energized with a zest for life and a more joy filled perspective.

Now that I've improved my eating habits to consuming more proteins, vegetables and fruits, healthy home cooking and eating less junk food, I am healthier, more upbeat, more energetic and focused at work because, thanks to my workouts, I am less stressed by work and life's concerns for the first time in my life. My sleep has improved dramatically, which restores my energy. There is even less of a desire to eat the junk foods, since there is no longer the emotional eating that was used to forget about the concerns that plagued me during the toughest times of my life. Who knew that joyful optimism actually makes one happier and stronger, able to endure hardships and improve one's health? What a major improvement! Thank You, Lord!

Everything that we experience and every person we meet has a purpose and a lesson to teach and give us. Pray and choose to be Joyful today regardless of your circumstances, which are allowed to instruct and strengthen you, polishing you into the diamond you were divinely designed to become with God's help. He will encourage and help you as you trust in and depend on Him. God knows exactly what you are feeling and He wants to have a conversation and a deeper relationship with you. He will advise and help you, so never stop praying. I Thessalonians 5:15-16 states, *"Rejoice always, pray continually, give thanks in all circumstances for this is God's will for you in Christ Jesus."* Also, James 1:2-4 enlightens us further: *"Consider it pure joy, my brothers and sisters, whenever you face trials of many kinds, because you know that the testing of your faith produces perseverance. Let perseverance finish its work so that you may be mature and complete, not lacking anything."*

Earlier in this section, I mentioned the hymn "His Eye is On the Sparrow." This song is inspired by the words of Jesus in the Gospel of Matthew 6:26 and Matthew 10:29-31: *"Look at the birds of the air; they neither sow nor reap nor gather into barns, and yet your heavenly Father feeds them. Are you not of more value than they?"* —Matthew 6:26

"Are not two sparrows sold for a farthing? and one of them shall not fall on the ground without your Father. But the very hairs of your head

are all numbered. Fear ye not therefore, ye are of more value than many sparrows."-Matthew 10:29-31 I was reading about Ethel Waters some years ago, from her autobiography, entitled by the name of this hymn. It was inspiring to learn the origin of the hymn, originally written in 1905 by two Caucasian songwriters, composer Charles H. Gabriel and lyricist Civilla D. Martin. Civilla had this to say when questioned about her sources of inspiration for the words of this song. In addition to the above scriptures, she explained:

"Early in the spring of 1905, my husband and I were sojourning in Elmira, New York. We contracted a deep friendship for a couple by the name of Mr. and Mrs. Doolittle—true saints of God. Mrs. Doolittle had been bedridden for nigh twenty years. Her husband was an incurable cripple who had to propel himself to and from his business in a wheel chair. Despite their afflictions, they lived happy Christian lives, bringing inspiration and comfort to all who knew them. One day while we were visiting with the Doolittles, my husband commented on their bright hopefulness and asked them for the secret of it. Mrs. Doolittle's reply was simple: "His eye is on the sparrow, and I know He watches me." The beauty of this simple expression of boundless faith gripped the hearts and fired the imagination of Dr. Martin and me. The hymn 'His Eye Is on the Sparrow' was the outcome of that experience.

The beauty of this expression of simple faith gripped my heart and that same evening I wrote the words for the song. The rest, as they say, is history. If you're discouraged, afraid of the future, or struggling with the problems of today, listen again to the words of this beautiful song: "Why should I feel discouraged? Why should the shadows come? Why should my heart feel lonely, and long for heaven and home? When Jesus is my portion, a constant friend is He. His eye is on the sparrow and I know He watches over me. His eye is on the sparrow; and I know He watches me. I sing because I'm happy. I sing because I'm free! His eye is on the sparrow; and I know He watches me. His eye is on the sparrow; and I know He watches me."
—Civilla D. Martin

These lyrics cause me to realize the difference between joy and happiness. Joy comes from inside the heart, knowing that God loves and cares for us. This knowledge does not rely on feeling happy about whatever has happened. Get it? Happiness relies on something happening, yet joy springs from within and endures no matter what your circumstances are. Certainly, one can choose to be joyful despite life's trials and challenges as James 1:2-3 points out, *"For you know that when your faith is tested, your endurance has a chance to grow."* As I heard a Sunday School teacher share many years ago, "Dealing with the unbearable is the beginning of the curve in the road to joy." So choose to be joyful! Allow your unbearable moments to bring you closer to the experience of God's ever present joy in your heart, for as Psalm 126:3 shares, *"The Lord has done great things for us, and we are filled with joy."* Joy is a fruit of the Holy Spirit's presence in your life: *"But the fruit of the Spirit is love, **joy**, peace, longsuffering, gentleness, goodness, faith, meekness, temperance: against such there is no law…If we live in the Spirit, let us also walk in the Spirit,"* Galatians 5:22-23, 25.

Did you know that joy is our natural state of being? Babies enter the joyful state so easily because they are fully in the present moment, instead of living in the past or in the future. Belief in God, and choosing to accept His gift of salvation to guide your daily life, help us to understand and see things in a different way from what the world presents to us. *"Believe in God; believe that He is, and that He created all things, both in heaven and in earth; believe that He has all wisdom, and all power, both in heaven and in earth; believe that man doth not comprehend all the things which the Lord can comprehend."* - Seeing and living in a Godly way, causes us to be happy and joyful in a far deeper way which only the Gospel of Jesus Christ can bring into one's life. That said, such a person is empowered to live according to His divine purpose. When you live a life of purpose, your relationship with time changes dramatically. Unlike others, you are not looking for happiness in the future, by saying things like, "When Y happens, then I will be happy and I'll be right where I've always wanted to be." No, instead you will be grateful in the present moment, thanking God for where you are, what you have and how things are better right here, right now. Herein you are saying, in effect, "Nothing could be more perfect than this present moment." Realize that the present is a gift. Be thankful for the gift! Where there is joy, there is inner peace.

So when you are faced with a decision, no matter how mundane it may be, choose what brings you closest to joy, for the joy of the Lord is the believer's strength, according to Nehemiah 8:10, and His Presence empowers you to be a victor rather than a victim, hopeful rather than one who suffers without hope. When you are joyful, life flows with lightness and ease, as you embrace with gratitude the life you live. God woke us up this morning, gave us a brand new day, filled with new mercies and opportunities. He led you to read this book, designed to uplift, encourage and strengthen you. Rejoice! Joyful feeling created joyful actions which produce more joyful feelings, so rejoice always, and again I say, rejoice! For in the words of Isaac Watts, penned in 1707:

"Come, we that love the Lord, and let our joys be known, join in a song with sweet accord, and thus surround the throne. Let those refuse to sing who never knew our God; but children of the heavenly King may speak their joys abroad. Then let our songs abound, and every tear be dry; we're marching through Emmanuel's ground to fairer worlds on high."

In this state of joy, empowered by Christ, we are enabled to stop worrying so much about our survival, as we trust in Him to help us. As for me, He gives me joy and makes my heart sing in praise. Through Him, we who are filled with His Spirit are enabled to be positive influencers of the world around us. Your focus will be on interacting daily without fear. People will be drawn to you like a magnet and your life will be filled with responsibly empowered relationships, to support others and be supported by others.

Many years ago, I taught a science lesson to my Sunday School class about overflowing joy as part of a unit on dealing with tough times in our lives. I used a 12 oz. clear drinking glass, a round cake pan; ½ cup of vinegar; one teaspoon of baking soda; one cup of water and five paper cups. I poured about 1/8 cup of water in three of the paper cups. I wrote the word "pray" on the side of one cup, "believe" on another paper cup and "Bible" on the third paper cup, and left the rest of the water for later use in this object lesson. Vinegar was poured in the fourth paper cup, where the words "Problems and Troubles" were written on the side of this paper cup. Baking soda was poured into the last paper cup and "Holy Spirit" was written on the side of that cup. Then I read to the class this passage of scripture in Philippians 4:4 which says, "Rejoice in the Lord always; again I will say, Rejoice."

God's Word tells us that we should always be joyful. This does not mean that we will always be happy, but we can still have joy, even when things aren't going well. When you trust in Jesus as your Savior His Spirit comes to live in you. The Holy Spirit produces fruit in your life as you listen to Him and you allow Him to control your thoughts, attitudes and actions. Joy is one of the fruits the Holy Spirit produces in your life. "But the fruit of the Spirit is love, joy, peace, patience, kindness, goodness, faithfulness, gentleness, self control…" according to Galatians 5:22-23 ESV.

When problems come into your life, Satan wants you to complain or worry and even doubt God; he wants to rob you of your joy. Remember, you have the Holy Spirit's power to win over Satan and be joyful even during hard times.

Today I have water, baking soda and vinegar. Now by mixing these three ingredients, something special happens that will help you remember to always have joy. Now this clear drinking glass represents your life. I will put the glass in the cake pan; (this is to catch the mixture when it overflows.) When you receive Jesus as your Savior, He comes to live inside of you by His Spirit. As I pour water into this glass, the water represents the fact that God's forgiveness washed away your sin and all of its punishment, so now you now have new life! (This is when I pour the water into the clear drinking glass until it is about half full.)

Next, the cup that has "Problems and Troubles" written on it is filled with vinegar. Did you know that vinegar is an acetic acid that

is a weak acid which can be eaten. Eating this does not harm your body, but it does add a sour taste to your food. Just because you have received Jesus does not mean that you will no longer have problems. This vinegar reminds me of problems and troubles. Even though vinegar has a sour taste, it can add a good flavor to food. Well, God uses problems and troubles in our lives to teach us to depend on Him so that only He gets our praise. Now when problems come, you might feel like complaining, worrying, or doubting God. (This is when I pour the vinegar into the clear drinking glass.) But don't allow these bad attitudes and feelings to rob you of your joy! Instead, allow the Holy Spirit to produce the fruit of joy in your life.

Here's a cup of water that has "Pray" written on it. When problems come, one of the first things you can do is pray. Tell God how you feel and thank Him that He is with you as you go through this hard time. God tells us in Jeremiah 33:3, "Call to me and I will answer you, and will tell you great and hidden things that you have not known." (This is when I pour the water from the "Pray" cup into the clear drinking glass.) Next, trust or believe that God will help you go through this tough time. Here is another cup of water with the word "Believe" written on it. Jesus said in Matthew 21:22, "And whatever you ask in prayer, you will receive, if you have faith." Faith and trust mean we are to believe in God and have confidence that God will do what He says. (This is when I pour the water from the "Believe" cup into the clear drinking glass.) You have just talked to God. Now is the time that you need to allow Him to talk to you. Look at this cup that has "Bible" written on it. Spend time reading God's Word and allowing Him to speak to you. The Book of Psalms has a lot to say about praising God during our troubles. Listen to Psalm 56:2-4 which says, "my enemies trample on me all day long, for many attack me proudly. When I am afraid, I put my trust in you. In God, whose word I praise, in God I trust; I shall not be afraid. What can flesh do to me?" (This is the time that I pour the water from the "Bible" cup into the clear drinking glass.)

So when you pray, believe and read the Bible. God's Spirit, living inside you will begin to change your thoughts and attitudes about the trouble or problem you are facing.

Here I have some baking soda in the cup that has the words "Holy Spirit" written on it. Now, watch what happens when I pour the baking soda into the water and vinegar mixture. (Now I pour the baking soda into the clear drinking glass. The liquid in the glass begins to bubble over.) This shows that when God's Spirit is controlling your thoughts and attitudes, then the fruit of joy will overflow in your life. When the vinegar mixes with the baking soda, the acetic acid in the vinegar neutralizes, or reduces the full

effect of the baking soda. Then a gas called carbon dioxide forms. Carbon dioxide is actually the bubbles that overflow when vinegar reacts with the baking soda. This baking soda reminds me of the joy that comes from the Holy Spirit as you obey God and trust in His promises. The fruit of joy that comes from God's

Spirit is a deep inner gladness you have because you know that God is in control. It's the inner gladness you have when you realize that God is faithful and always keeps His promises. Through His Spirit, God will give you His joy and strength to handle life's problems. In the Bible we read, "Do not grieve or be sad, for the joy of the Lord is your strength," according to Nehemiah 8:10. So, the next time you are facing a problem, please remember what happens when you add baking soda to vinegar. May each of you allow the fruit of joy to overflow in your life!

So choose to fulfill your mission in life, as God speaks to your heart, making decisions that strengthen your joy. In the words of the Twila Paris lyrics, "The Joy of the Lord will be my Strength; I will not falter, I will not faint; He is my Shepherd, I am not afraid; the Joy of the Lord is my Strength." Listen to the Scriptures that promise joy, and see why my heart is continuously so filled with joy:

*I will greatly **rejoice** in the Lord, my soul shall be **joyful** in my God; for*

He has clothed me with the garments of salvation, He has covered me with the robe of righteousness, as a bridegroom decks Himself with ornaments, and as a bride adorns herself with jewels. Isaiah 61:10

*The Lord is my strength and my shield; my heart trusts in Him and He helps me. My heart leaps for **joy** and with my song I praise Him. The Lord is their strength, and He is the saving strength of His anointed. Psalm 28:7-8*

*For the **joy** of the Lord is your strength. Nehemiah 8:10b*

*I will bless the Lord at all times: His praise shall continually be in my mouth. My soul shall make her boast in the Lord: the humble shall hear and be **glad**. Psalm 34:1, 2*

*But let all those that put their trust in You **rejoice**: let them ever shout for **joy,** because You defend them: let them also that love Your Name be **joyful** in You. Psalm 5:11*

*You will show me the path of life: in Your presence is fullness of **joy**; at Your right hand, there are pleasures forevermore. Psalm 16:11*

*But You are **joy**, O You that inhabits the praises of Israel. Psalm 22:3*

*Weeping may endure for a night, but **joy** comes in the morning. Psalm 30:5*

*Your Words were found, and I did eat them; and Your Word was unto me the **joy** and **rejoicing** of my heart: for I am called by Your Name, O Lord God of Hosts. Jeremiah 15:16*

*But the fruit of the Spirit is love, **joy**, peace, longsuffering, gentleness, goodness, faith, meekness, temperance: against such there is no law…If we live in the Spirit, let us also walk in the Spirit. Galatians 5:22-23, 25*

***Rejoice** in the Lord always: and again I say, **Rejoice**. Philippians 4:4*

***Rejoice** evermore. I Thessalonians 5:16*

*My brethren, count it all **joy** when you fall into divers temptations. James 1:2*

*Let us be **glad** and **rejoice**, and give honor to Him: for the marriage of the Lamb is come, and His wife has made herself read. Revelations 19:7*

Let the words of Henry Van Dyke's 1907 hymn, composed to the music of Ludwig van Beethoven in 1824 speak to your heart when you need to be uplifted. In fact, the words were written by a great clergyman, poet and English literature educator of the 19th century who was a graduate of both Princeton University and Princeton Theological Seminary. Now Beethoven never wrote any hymns, however the music for this hymn comes from Beethoven's Ninth Symphony, since various people adapted portions of his music to serve as hymn tunes. Mr. Van Dyke was delighted by the joyful sound of Beethoven's Ninth. Therefore, he thought this should be used as a hymn tune, for he was well known for his devotional writings and seized by the visual beauty of the surrounding mountains while he was a guest preacher at Williams College in Massachusetts. That said, let the words of this inspirational hymn minister to you, for as I John 4:16 states, *"God is love, and those who abide in love abide in God, and God abides in them."*

Joyful, joyful, we adore Thee, God of glory, Lord of love;

hearts unfold like flowers before Thee, opening to the sun above.

Melt the clouds of sin and sadness, drive the dark of doubt away;

Giver of immortal gladness, fill us with the light of day!

All Thy works with joy surround Thee, earth and heaven reflect Thy rays,

Stars and angels sin around Thee, Center of unbroken praise.

Field and forest, vale and mountain, flowery meadow, flashing sea,

Chanting bird and flowing fountain call us to rejoice in Thee.

Thou are giving and forgiving, ever blessing, ever blest,

Wellspring of the joy of living, ocean depth of happy rest!

Thou our Father, Christ our Brother, all who live in love are Thine;

Teach us how to love each other, lift us to the Joy Divine.

We each need to realize that life is a priceless gift from God. He designed us to live life to the fullest, or as one lyricist expressed, to "live life like it's golden." That means that we are to lead a life that is productive, rich and vibrant. Instead of looking for gray clouds in the sky, look for the silver lining in the clouds. Look for the best aspect of situations and people. Awaken to each new day with a song in your heart, ready to discover the rewards of living. This is what is meant by living optimistically, for in doing so, the optimist has a tendency to see the bigger picture rather than the minutia. As an optimist, I am driven by purposeful living, as evidenced by my checklist of aspirations, or as some call may call it, a vision board. After all, where there is no vision, there is no success in attaining one's goals. I appreciate the simple things in life. I have an immense respect for humanity as well as opportunities. For me, life is more about creating and treasuring memorable moments as I sojourn in this pilgrimage through life. To that end, here are some practical strategies to employ in your life in order that you may live more joyfully.

1. Silence and Stillness are Golden

We are surrounded by too much meaningless noise. However, we can turn down the volume on all the noise in our lives. In doing so, we will discover the amazing fact that silence and stillness are already here and have been here the whole time. When we daily and purposefully allow ourselves to be still, we naturally open up to a deeper appreciation of the present moment. We will become relaxed, more grounded and clearer. All of the stress will begin to melt away.

What can you do today to bring silence into your life? When will you choose to just stop and be still?

2. Clean It Up Now

Recently I saw a television program that was dedicated to people whose homes and garages were filled with clutter. What a shame to observe such a tragedy because each person in that situation expressed their disgust, frustration, tendency to procrastinate and their resulting lack of joy. When I see clutter forming in my life, I schedule some time to get rid of it. I have several spring cleanings during the year to eliminate what is no longer needed, reorganize what is needed, and reflect on the best place to put it. Some of my wardrobe is in the garage to accommodate what is seasonal and necessary in my closet. If something is suddenly needed for whatever reason, I go shopping in the garage. What a treat! Also, it's very cost effective. Lately, I noticed that I had been out of touch with due to commitments, so I scheduled a get together with key people and started texting or emailing the rest as time permitted. As much as I like Facebook's ability to stay in touch with the wonderful people in my life, it requires more time than I have to keep up with the myriad comments that are posted, so I do that only as I am able. Next, I looked at how I am using the time and talents I am gifted with recently and realized that all work and no creativity is very dissatisfying. So I stopped making excuses and busily began to write as inspirations came to me.

So if there is any area in your life that you procrastinate about, pay attention and fix it. Find out what needs to be done to resolve the issue. Carve out the time, find the best solution, make yourself a committee of one and clean it up. This is how you make the space for joy and peace to illuminate your life.

3. Mind your own business

The most frustrating unhappiness I've experienced came from and trying to control people and situations that I am unable to actually do anything positive about. It is what it is. I've learned to shut up, pray and move forward, for silence is golden. Lord knows my intentions were good though with more wisdom than I had at the time, things could have been done better. I've done the best I could, where and when I could, and with His help, I continue to live, grow and give for His utmost pleasure. My mistakes have taught me volumes. Where I've erred, He has forgiven me, and I have forgiven myself as well as others. Enough said. The past is gone, so I cannot change that, yet I can learn from it and live better from those lessons. I realize that cannot change people unless they decide to be changed because they each have free will or the right to choose. However, I can do what I need to do to be the best me that I can be and do the most good. When I change, everything around me automatically changes. That is my sphere of influence where I choose to make the most difference with God's guidance. Now, look at yourself. If you are caught in a situation or in an emotional reaction, turn the mirror onto yourself to face your part in how it came about. Let go of the drama. Let go of your need to control and let God help you. See what is actually true and learn from your mistakes. Bring compassion where it is most needed. Diligently work on the areas where you get stuck. Then joy will shine through you.

4. Give to Others

Our world is so focused on being needy for time, attention, love, and understanding. More, more, more is the outcry. When one lives in a state of lack, one tends to think that life only begins when one gets what is needed. Change your choice. Instead of living in lack, consider generosity. When you are giving, you are living by giving to others what you want or need. Pour yourself out by offering genuine attention, listening to others, showing interest, and caring for others' needs. You will become satisfied due to being transformed by sharing love with others.

5. Use All of Your Senses

This joyful, abundant life is right here for us to partake of, so slow down and be more observant, enjoying the moments as they come.

Take the time to touch, see, hear, taste and smell the world around you, savoring it as you do. Even eating an peach becomes a sensual delight in this process, as you gratefully experience a symphony of enjoyment.

6. Take Stock of What is Working for You

It is too easy to focus on problems and feeling discontent. Stop allowing this negative energy to grab your attention. Negativity will not let go once you give in to it, for it is just as tenacious as a dog feasting on a juicy bone. I was driving to work one day, and just as I was about to cross the green light, I was delayed by a tiny dog in the middle of my lane. That little Chihuahua mixed breed was feasting on a meaty bone it had found right there in the street! The cars in front of me were honking at it yet I could not see what they were honking at until they had gone around it.

That's what negative energy is like, except it is gnawing on your mind, sapping your positive energy. So take charge. Take stock of what is working for good in your life. Do you enjoy your work? Is it your passion that you just love to get up and do? Is your living situation a good one? Do you know people who you love and appreciate? Do you enjoy your daily runs or a good home-cooked meal? Simply look around you and you may be surprised by the abundant bounty that is already present.

7. Love and Live, Be Willing to Forgive

Whether in love or just in life, issues do arise. When a grudge or difficulty interferes with your joy of life, then it requires your loving attention. Let not the issues or grudges multiply by the minutes ticking by. Let not your life be steeped regrets, doubts or self-righteousness. You be the bigger person if need be and start the process. Make amends sooner rather than later. When you feel wronged by someone or you hurt another, deal with it instead of letting it fester for when you forgive, you are set free to live joyfully. Neutralize the stories from the past, and make the choice to live joyfully now. You will be strengthened and empowered.

8. Learn from All of Life's Experiences

Sometimes the road of life is a bumpy one. If you want to master joyful living, be open to learning from life's challenges. Be honest about what pushes your buttons. Recognize when you have dropped into some quicksand that you can't seem to find your way out of. Difficult life experiences are designed to show us the areas in our lives where we are not yet free. Use these situations well for your own liberation, for the teachings keep coming until we finally understand the lesson. If you observe any self-defeating patterns in your life, slow things down so that you can become more aware of what you are doing and the catalysts that bring those reactions about. Choose to be proactive rather than reactive. Set the necessary boundaries in your life. Then you can make far better choices with your eyes wide open.

9. Be Pleasingly Pleasant

A pleasant perspective makes life more agreeable. No matter what is going on in your life, show up in an open, good-natured way. Choose to be positive and optimistic. No one likes a Negative Nancy. Stop complaining! Instead be patient, loving, open, kind, and agreeable, both in your daily life and in all interactions.

10. Decide to Drive in the Direction of Joy

Every moment offers a choice. Look at your life and your behavior to observe what you truly value. Are you choosing stress, conflict, and unhappiness, or peace, stillness and joy? Joy provides an excellent barometer for navigating through life. Recognize what brings you joy, then follow it. Make room in your life for what is full of light, optimism and purpose. This is the way to master the art of joyful living.

BE FRUITFUL

Taste the Best Fruit Ever:
Developing the Fruits of God's Spirit

There is something so refreshing and invigorating about the taste of a fruit: simple, sweet, natural, healthy, fragrant and nourishing. Well, the Bible reveals that there are nine spiritually healthy fruits evidenced in the lives of those who have God's Holy Spirit within them. Do you see these traits in your life? Are you growing in them? Suppose you were put on trial, "accused" of being a Christian. How would the prosecution build their case either for or against you? What evidence could they present as proof of your "guilt," that is, what proof is there of you being a Christ follower, a believer, a Christian? The bottom line of that question is ultimately summed up like this: How can you know for certain that you have God's Holy Spirit dwelling in you? How can others know that the Holy Spirit is working in you? First and foremost, the apostle Paul showed that it is only the Holy Spirit dwelling in your mind that makes you a Christian: *"But you are not in the flesh, but in the Spirit, if so be that the Spirit of God dwell in you. Now if any man have not the Spirit of Christ, he is none of His,"* according to Romans 8:9. Since having the Spirit of God live inside you is the prerequisite for being a Christian, there must be traits or qualities we can see in ourselves that reflect our spiritual state.

Comparably, there are traits in true Christians today, as specified in the book of Revelations, chapter 3, verses 1-22, demonstrated traits that determine whether Christians are like Sardis, the spiritually dead church of West Asia Minor that was more concerned material things instead of spiritual things; Philadelphian, the faithful church; or like the lukewarm Laodicean church, which was neither faithful nor true to the things of Christ. Consequently, there are characteristics that we all must exhibit in our daily lifestyles in order to even be considered by God to be a part of the living body of Christ.

Take notice of what the apostle Paul was inspired to write in Galatians 5:22-23: *"But the fruit of the Spirit is love, joy, peace, longsuffering, gentleness, goodness, faith, meekness, temperance: against such there is no law."* These are areas of spiritual living in which we all must be growing daily as we strive to overcome our three main enemies: 1) Satan, as referred to in James 4:7, which states, *"Submit yourselves, then, to God. Resist the devil and he will flee from you;"* 2) the world , as noted in James 4:4, *"You adulterous people, don't you know that friendship with the world is hatred toward God? Anyone who chooses to be a friend of the world becomes an enemy of God. Or do you think Scripture says without reason that the Spirit He caused to live in us envies intensely?;"* and, 3), our own human nature, as explained in Romans 8:7-9, *"the sinful mind is hostile to God. It does not submit to God's law, nor can it do so. Those controlled by the sinful nature cannot please God. You, however, are controlled not by the sinful nature, but by The [Holy] Spirit, if the Spirit of God lives in you."*

Now, let us fully examine what it means to have and be controlled by these qualities and how they affect our relationship with God as well as our fellowman. Let us notice how growth in these key areas will ultimately determine our eternal reward in God's kingdom.

Love

Love is the first fruit that Paul lists as evidence that God's Spirit is working in a person's mind. What does it mean to have love? The world's "Christian" churches universally teach the false concept of love, that is, the concept that love is reduced to a mere feeling, just a hollow emotional expression that is punctuated with words that tend to have meaning only during certain times of the year. Such churches are teaching that God's "harsh law" was done away by Christ's sacrifice, so they claim that in order to be a Christian, all that one needs to have is the feeling of love.

Conversely, how does God define true Christian love? Well, there are actually many aspects of love, which is expressed in the original

33

Greek language as agape. First, notice Christ's words in John 15:13, *"Greater love has no man than this, that a man lay down his life for his friends."* Herein, Christ showed that the ultimate expression of Godly love is the willingness of sacrifice, to voluntarily put one's own life on the line for others.

Moreover, notice the clarification of Ephesians 5:29, *"For no man ever yet hated his own flesh; but nourishes and cherishes it, even as the Lord the church." In other words, to exercise true Godly love is to go against the natural human instinct of self-preservation, putting the concerns of others above our own"* as noted by Philippians 2:3. When giving what has popularly become known as "the Golden Rule," Jesus Christ exhorted in Mark 12:31, *"And the second is like, namely this, You shall love your neighbor as yourself."* Also in John 13:35, Christ said, *"By this shall all men know that you are My disciples, if you have love one to another."*

Joy

The second fruit of the Holy Spirit is joy. Speaking to His disciples, Christ said, "These things have I spoken unto you, that My joy might remain in you, and that your joy might be full" (John 15:11). In the Greek language, the word joy is translated as chara, which means cheerfulness, calm delight and gladness.

How do you know that you are evidencing joy in your life? Do you face your trials with gladness, cheerfulness and calm delight? This should be our daily mindset throughout our Christian walk. Notice how Paul emphasizes this attribute in Hebrews 1:9 by stating, *"You have loved righteousness, and hated iniquity; therefore God, even your God, has anointed you with the oil of gladness above your fellows."*

Now, in the parable of the talents, read Christ's words in Matthew 25:14-30: *"His lord said unto him, Well done, you good and faithful servant: you have been faithful over a few things, I will make you ruler over many things: enter you into the JOY of your lord."* As Christians, we are being judged daily according to what we do, with what we have, in the amount of time that we have. Therefore, those who grow and overcome in this lifetime, by being faithful stewards of the gifts that God has given them, will ultimately enter into *"the joy of the Lord."*

Peace

The third evidence of having God's Holy Spirit working within you is peace. In John 14:27, Christ said to His disciples, *"Peace I leave with you, My peace I give unto you: not as the world gives, give I unto you. Let not your heart be troubled, neither let it be afraid."*

This word peace is translated from the Greek word eirene, meaning "rest, peace and quietness." Christians are those who remain peaceful through difficult trials and the sundry negative circumstances that occur in their lives. In fact, Christ showed that we are to be active promoters of peace by saying in Matthew 5:9, *"Blessed are the peacemakers: for they shall be called the children of God."* So, as Christians, we must strive to maintain peaceful relationships with others, turning the other cheek when we are wronged as clarified in Matthew 5:39 and Luke 6:29. Also, as Psalm 34:14 shows, we are to *"Depart from evil, and do good; seek peace, and pursue it."*

Longsuffering

The fourth characteristic seen in the lives of true Christians is called longsuffering. This simply means "Suffering long," enduring through trials. Of course, this requires a great degree of patience in order to always remember the words of Romans 8:28 that states, *"all things work together for good to them that love God, to them who are called according to His purpose."*

Somehow, there are some people who wrongly confuse longsuffering with patience. While the Bible does emphasize the need for God's people to exercise patience, this only becomes longsuffering if one waits while enduring some kind of pain: in other words, this typifies patience under duress. It is through suffering for an extended period of time that you can develop patience, in waiting for God to work things out in His own time and in His own way. In chapter 5, verse 10, the apostle James wrote, *"Take, my brethren, the prophets, who have spoken in the name of the Lord, for an example of suffering affliction, and of patience."*

Also, notice what Christ said in Matthew 24:23, *"Then if any man shall say unto you, Lo, here is Christ, or there; believe it not."* Those who pray "Thy kingdom come" must exercise and grow in both wisdom and patience, while discerning the "signs of the times," watching and praying always, in order not to be among those deceived by false ministers and false christs. Always be on guard against the possibility of becoming impatient for Christ's Return, as well as the binding of Satan, and the establishment of the kingdom of God. We must always remember that in Matthew 24:36, Christ Himself says that He does not know the exact "day and hour" of His Return. So, beware anyone who declares that they actually know the specific hour and day when Jesus Christ will return.

Furthermore, notice in Revelation 3:10: *"Because you have kept the word of My patience, I also will keep you from the hour of temptation, which shall come upon all the world, to try them that dwell upon the earth."* The New King James version translates the phrase, "the word of My patience" as "My command to persevere" for this helps to better convey the full meaning. Other scripture verses, noted below, show how patience, endurance and perseverance are vital in our Christian lives, especially in the end time, when world conditions will be worse than they have ever been. Read the following scriptures:

Matthew 10:22: *"And you shall be hated of all men for My name's sake: but he that endures to the end shall be saved."*

Acts 14:22: *"Confirming the souls of the disciples, and exhorting them to continue in the faith, and that we must through much tribulation enter into the kingdom of God."*

Revelation 13:10: *"…Here is the patience and faith of the saints."*

Revelation 14:12: *"Here is the patience of the saints: here are they that keep the commandments of God, and the faith of Jesus."*

Luke 21:19: *"In your patience possess you your souls [lives]."*

Daniel 12:12: *"Blessed is he that waits..."*

These verses all show the importance of patience through longsuffering in the lives of those who are *"called according to [God's] purpose"* as Romans 8:28 enlightens. Also, in Matthew 24:13, Christ said, *"But he that shall endure unto the end, the same shall be saved."*

Gentleness

The fifth fruit of the Holy Spirit is gentleness. What does it mean to be gentle? The Greek word used in Galatians 5 is chrestotes, which means "gentleness, goodness and kindness." To grasp what this means in the life of a Christian, first notice Paul's words in I Thessalonians 2:7: *"But we were gentle among you, even as a nurse cherishes her children."* Here, Paul is showing one aspect of his role as a minister, which mirrors what Christ said in Matthew 23:37: *"O Jerusalem, Jerusalem, you that kills the prophets, and stones them which are sent unto you, how often would I have gathered your children together, even as a hen gathers her chickens under her wings, and you would not!"*

To be gentle is to realize that we all require a certain degree of "handling with care." It means to deal with people in such a way as to take their needs and feelings into consideration, understanding that, just as you have certain sensitivities, others are also sensitive in various ways.

Goodness

The sixth trait seen in a true Christian is goodness. Ephesians 5:9 states, *"For the fruit of the Spirit is in all goodness and righteousness and truth;"* The word used here in the Greek is agathosune, meaning "goodness...virtue or beneficence." Webster's Dictionary defines beneficence as "doing or producing good; especially: performing acts of kindness and charity."

This trait is also summed up in Matthew 5:44: *"But I say unto you, Love your enemies, bless them that curse you, DO GOOD to them that hate you, and pray for them which despitefully use you, and persecute you."*

Christ further expounded upon this in Luke 6:31-35: *"And as you would that men should do to you, DO YOU ALSO TO THEM LIKEWISE. For if you love them which love you, what thank have you? For sinners also love those that love them. And if you do good to them which do good to you, what thank have you? For sinners also do even the same. And if you lend to them of whom you hope to receive, what thank have you? For sinners also lend to sinners, to receive as much again. But love you your enemies, and DO GOOD, and lend, hoping for nothing again; and your reward shall be great, and you shall be the children of the Highest: for He is kind unto the unthankful and to the evil."*

Christ is showing that one of the tests of true conversion is whether or not we can show goodness to those who are not naturally inclined to show goodness to us in return. This goes directly against human nature, which tends to seek vengeance and retribution for wrongdoing. We must continue to grow in this area so that we can ultimately hear Christ say in Matthew 25:21, *"Well done, you good and faithful servant…"*

Faith

The seventh fruit of God's Spirit is faith, which is also listed as a gift of the same Holy Spirit in I Corinthians 12:9. In Hebrews 11:6, Paul writes, *"Without faith, it is impossible to please God"* yet what is faith? In verse 1, faith is defined as *"the substance of things hoped for, the evidence of things not seen."* In other words, faith is its own proof of the validity and certainty of God's promises to us. It is our proof that God will honor, fulfill and make good on His words. It is our proof that He will intervene in our trials. By faith, we can be assured that God will not require us to endure more suffering than we can bear, according to I Corinthians 10:13. For further clarification, in

the Greek language, the word translated as faith in Galatians 5:23 is the word pistis, which actually means, moral conviction, persuasion and credence… especially reliant on Jesus Christ for salvation. That means we have to place our complete trust in God, for as Philippians 1:6 shares, *"Being confident…that He which has begun a good work in you will perform it until the day of Jesus Christ."* It takes faith to endure until the end (see Matthew 10:22), realizing that God will *"never leave you nor forsake you"* as He promised in Hebrews 13:5.

Meekness

As the eighth fruit of God's Holy Spirit, meekness, or praotes in the Greek, meaning "gentleness, humility" is a quality that is often viewed by others as weakness. Most people would consider a meek individual as one who is easily swayed, or a "pushover."

Notice how God describes Moses, a man whom He used to perform mighty miracles in delivering Israel out of slavery and leading them to the Promised Land:

"Now the man Moses was very meek, above all the men which were upon the face of the earth." - Numbers 12:3

So, meekness is not a lack of strength. It is an attitude of approaching God and our neighbor through humility, realizing from John 5:19, 30 that we can do nothing apart from God, but that, through Christ, we can do ALL things according to Philippians 4:13.

Temperance

The ninth fruit of God's Holy Spirit, TEMPERANCE (from the Greek word egkrateia, meaning "self-control"), is a quality that is clearly lacking in today's society. From eating disorders to "road rage" to violence in schools, the evidence of the lack of self-control is everywhere. Those who do have God's Spirit dwelling in their minds should be exercising control over their emotions and actions, not *"giving place to the devil"* (Eph. 4:27) and this should be obvious to those around us. We should not allow circumstances or situations to dictate our mood, demeanor or language. Rather, Christians should remain in control of their emotions and attitudes, remembering that *"There has no temptation taken you but such as is common to man: but God is faithful, who will not suffer you to be tempted above that you are able; but will with the temptation also make a way to escape, that you may be able to bear it"* (I Cor. 10:13).

So here is the final verdict, as referenced earlier in my earlier analogy. If you are evidencing these nine fruits in your life, the jury hearing your case should be able to hand down a verdict of "Guilty" on the charge of being a Christian. You should be able to *"have a good conscience; that, whereas they speak evil of you, as of evildoers, they may be ashamed that falsely accuse your good conversation [conduct] in Christ"* as noted in I Peter 3:16. Also, having these spiritual fruits enables those who possess them to live sunny side up, realizing that Christ is our All in All.

BE GRATEFUL

It is a good thing to give thanks unto the LORD, and to sing praises unto Thy Name, O Most High: To shew forth Thy lovingkindness in the morning, and Thy faithfulness every night, upon an instrument of ten strings, and upon the psaltery; upon the harp with a solemn sound. For Thou, LORD, has made me glad through Thy work: I will triumph in the works of Thy hands. O LORD, how great are Thy works, and Thy thoughts are very deep. —Psalm 93:1-5

These days, it is far more likely to hear complaints rather than expressions of appreciation to God. Having "an attitude of gratitude" is a phrase that used to be exclusively devoted to praising the Lord, yet nowadays it is frequently used as a term to be "in alignment with the universe." Yet as Psalm 95:2 declares, *"Let us come before His Presence with thanksgiving."* Clearly, giving thanks to God is what true gratitude is originally and properly about. So many of us typically lead such hectic lives that any expression of thanksgiving is usually relegated to mealtime prayers. Oh, we may manage to squeeze in the time to ask God for our laundry list of sundry demands, yet how often do we pause just to say, "Thank You" to God, our Almighty Creator?

After all, the Bible instructs us that giving thanks should be a lifestyle, for this is where the concept of having an attitude of gratitude originated. First and foremost in our thoughts each day should be a prayer of thanks. According to Colossians 3:1-7, we are told, *"And whatever you do, whether in word or in deed, do it all in the name of the Lord Jesus, giving thanks to God the Father through Him."* In Psalm 103:2, the psalmist declares, *"bless the Lord, O my soul, and forget not all His benefits"* and in Ephesians 5:20, we are encouraged to always *"give thanks to God the Father for everything, in the Name of our Lord Jesus Christ."*

For me, one of my favorite times of the year is Thanksgiving since it is the one occasion that people stop and audibly express their thanks to the Lord. However, being grateful is something that is to be done all year long, day in and day out. This is God's desire for our lives, according to I Thessalonians 5:17: *"In everything, we are to give thanks, for this is God's will for you in Christ Jesus"* for James 1:17 shares that *"Every good and perfect gift is from above, coming down from the Father of the heavenly lights, Who does not change like shifting shadows. He chose to give us birth through the Word of truth, that we might be a kind of first fruits of all He created."*

It is through a grateful mindset that we are enabled to see our relationship with the Lord in the proper perspective, and understand how greatly we need God in every aspect of our lives. Let us therefore stay humble before Him and bless His name as we focus on developing a heart of thanksgiving in the ways we think, speak, pray and live.

Why should we give thanks to God? How should we praise Him? Primarily because, as Psalm 92:1-2 states, *"It is good to give thanks to the Lord, and to sing praises to Your Name, O Most High; To declare Your loving kindness in the morning, and Your faithfulness every night..."* Throughout the Bible, many examples are given to demonstrate the benefits and reasons for having an attitude of gratitude. In fact, King David regularly expressed a grateful heart toward his Creator, and this endeared him to God, as well as to many believers even to this present day. David often expressed his praise and thanks to the King of Kings, and Lord of Lords. We would do well to follow David's wonderful example. For those I have encountered along life's path who either expressed that they do not believe in God, or asked what they had to be thankful for, I provide this partial list of enlightenment along with a scriptural reference.

Give thanks to God for:

Your body —Psalm 139:14-16

God's many blessings and benefits —Psalm 68:19

For not staying angry with us and never giving up on us —Psalm 30:5

God's unfailing mercy and kindness Psalm 18:49, 86:13, —Psalm 108:4, 145:8-9

The joy God gives you in His Presence —Psalm 16:11

When you were in trouble, God heard all your many cries for help —Psalm 22:24, 18:6

God's faithfulness —Psalm 71:22

All God's marvelous works —Psalm 9:1, 111:2-4, 66:3-7, 72:18

Salvation —Psalm 16:9-11, 96:2, Psalm 71:23, 92:1

The hope God has given you —Psalm 16:9

For filling the earth with His love and goodness —Psalm 33:5

God's power —Psalm 29:3-10, 21:13

Deliverance —Psalm 18:49, 68:20

God is great and worthy of praise —Psalm 145:3, 96:4, Psalm 48:1

For listening to your prayers —Psalm 28:6, 116:1-2

For always being truthful —Psalm 33:2, 57:10, Psalm 117:2

Creation of the stars —Psalm 19:1-4

God's many and deep thoughts —Psalm 139:17-18

For preserving our ancestors —Psalm 22:4-5

God's judgments and warnings they provide you —Psalm 19:7-8, Psalm 119:164

God's laws and commands —Psalm 48:11, Psalm 112:1

God's righteousness and holiness —Psalm 30:4, Psalm 48:10, Psalm 99:3

How Should We Thank God?

Thank Him with your mouth, not just in your mind —Psalm 63:5, Psalm 51:15

Thank God continuously —Psalm 79:13, Psalm 75:9

Tell people about God's wondrous works —Psalm 96:3, Psalm 26:7

Sing praises to God, make it glorious —Psalm 101:1, Psalm 66:2

Even sing for joy in your bed —Psalm 149:5

Be glad and rejoice in God —Psalm 9:2

Fear God, honor/glorify Him, revere Him —Psalm 22:23

Stand in awe of God —Psalm 33:8

Lift up your hands to Him —Psalm 63:4

Think about God at night —Psalm 63:6

Thank Him with all your heart —Psalm 86:12, 138:1

Praise Him with dancing —Psalm 150:3, 149:3

Encourage others to praise/thank God —Psalm 67:3-5

Therefore, every day is Thanksgiving for Christians. Even in problems, we know, according to Romans 8:28 that God is *"working all things together for His good,"* even though we are going through trials just like the Apostle Paul experienced, yet he said in 2 Corinthians 7:4, *"I am exceedingly joyful in all our tribulation."* God will allow the storms of life, to grow you deeper in His Word and in the faith. I recall a story of a man who was watching a butterfly that was just struggling to exit its cocoon. Deciding to help it, the man took out his razor blade and

44

carefully slit the edge of the cocoon. Now, that butterfly finally escaped from its problematic exit, then immediately died. You see, God uses the struggle to cause the butterfly's heart to beat faster and pump blood into its wings. Likewise, our trials serve a valid purpose, making us struggle to develop our faith in God and enable us to spread our wings in gratitude, as we realize God's loving hand upon our lives. We rejoice that even in the lion's den or in the bull's pen, God' help is reliable, deepening our joy. He has kept and given us so many exceeding great and precious promises. Thank God continually for He is good.

I am reminded of the story of an old farmer whose ungodly relative paid him a visit. At the table, the farmer bowed his head and thanked God for the food that they were about to eat. The ungodly relative rudely asked, "What did you do that for? There is no God. We live in an age of enlightenment." To that the old farmer replied, "Well, there is one on the farm who does not thank God before he eats." The relative sat up and said, "Who is this fully enlightened one?" The farmer quietly replied, "My pig," which silenced the relative. Therein lies the reward for an ungrateful heart!

Far back in time, on September 6, 1620, the Pilgrims left Plymouth, England in search of both civil and religious liberty as they travelled for over two months through harsh storms at sea to land in Massachusetts in late November. After praying, the Pilgrims built hasty shelters. Sadly, due to being unprepared for the illness and starvation of a harsh winter in New England, almost half of them died before spring. Through the help of the Indians, as the Pilgrims persevered in prayer, they reaped an abundant harvest the following summer, after which they declared a three day feast that began on December 13, 1621. They thanked God for their survival and for their new Indian friends. Although Thanksgiving services were annually held in Virginia as early as 1607, this was America's first Thanksgiving Festival. It was Pilgrim Edward Winslow who described the Pilgrims' Thanksgiving as follows:

"Our harvest being gotten in, our Governor sent four men on fowling, i.e. bird hunting, so that we might, after a special manner, rejoice together after we had gathered the fruit of our labors. They four in one day killed as much fowl as...served the company almost a week...Many of the Indians [came] amongst us and ... their greatest Kin, Massasoit, with some ninety men, whom for three days we entertained and feasted; and they went out and killed five deer, which they brought...And although it be not always so plentiful as it was at this time with us, yet BY THE GOODNESS OF GOD WE ARE...FAR FROM WANT."

Subsequently, President George Washington and President Abraham Lincoln issued their respective Proclamations of Thanksgiving. Lincoln's original proclamation came in 1863 after the Battle of Gettysburg, which resulted in the loss of about 60,000 lives. After four months passed, it was in November that Abraham Lincoln delivered his famous "Gettysburg Address." Later, while walking among the thousands of graves there at Gettysburg, Lincoln committed his life to Jesus Christ. He shared with a friend, "When I left Springfield to assume the Presidency, I asked the people to pray for me. I was not a Christian. When I buried my son, the severest trial of my life, I was not a Christian. But when I went to Gettysburg and saw the graves of thousands of our soldiers, I then and there consecrated myself to Christ." Afterwards, Lincoln wrote this proclamation which eventually led to the establishment of our national Thanksgiving celebration. I share it here, for it speaks volumes about gratitude.

Proclamation of Thanksgiving
By the President of the United States of America

The year that is drawing toward its close has been filled with the blessings of fruitful years and healthful skies. To these bounties, which are so constantly enjoyed that we are prone to forget the Source from which they come, others have been added which are of so extraordinary a nature that they cannot fail to penetrate and soften even the heart which is habitually insensible to the ever-watchful providence of Almighty God.

In the midst of a civil war of unequaled magnitude and severity, which has sometimes seemed to foreign states to invite and to provoke their aggression, peace has been preserved with all nations, order has been maintained, the laws have been respected and obeyed, and harmony has prevailed everywhere, except in the theater of military conflict, while that theater has been greatly contracted by the advancing armies and navies of the Union.

Needful diversions of wealth and of strength from the field of peaceful industry to the national defense have not arrested the ploy, the shuttle, or the ship; the ax has enlarged the borders of our settlements, and the mines, as well of iron and coal as of the precious metals, have yielded even more abundantly than theretofore. Population has steadily increased notwithstanding the waste that has been made in the camp, the siege, and the battlefield, and the country, rejoicing in the consciousness of augmented strength and vigor, is permitted to expect continuance of years with large increase of freedom.

No human counsel hath devised nor hath any mortal hand worked out these great things. They are the gracious gifts of the Most High God, Who, while dealing with un in anger for our sins, hath nevertheless remembered mercy.

It has seemed to me fit and proper that they should be solemnly, reverently, and gratefully acknowledged, as with one heart and one voice, by the whole American people. I do therefore invite my fellow-citizens in every part of the United States, and also those who are at sea and those who are sojourning in foreign lands, to set apart and observe the last Thursday of November next as a day of Thanksgiving and praise to our beneficent Father Who dwelleth in the heavens. And I recommend to them that while offering up the ascriptions justly due to Him for such singular deliverances and blessings they do also, with humble penitence for our national perverseness and disobedience, commend to His tender care all those who have become widows, orphans, mourners, or sufferers in the lamentable civil strife in which we are unavoidably engaged, and fervently implore the interposition of the Almighty Hand to heal the wounds of the nation and to restore it, as soon as may be consistent with the Divine purposes, to the full enjoyment of peace, harmony, tranquility and union.

In testimony whereof I have hereunto set my hand and caused the seal of the United States to be affixed.

[Signed]

A. Lincoln

BE FLAVORFUL

Make Your Life Like Nutella

It is not about me, nor is it about you. It is about the Masterpiece. Life is about God at work in us, through us, around us, impacting others for the greatest good, which is living in fulfillment of His divine purpose. So do good to all the people.

It is what it is. Just do what you are supposed to do. Be who you are designed to be, or as it is often said these days, "just do you." Personally, to do you means to live optimistically, trusting God, Who leads us graciously and safely along life's journey. This is what I have learned in answer to my many "Why?' queries. Whatever has happened, was designed to teach you some vital lessons. Learn those lessons. Get stronger. Push your boundaries to grow into the next level. Live in such a way as to never make the same mistakes again. Teach by example. After all, look where God has already brought you from! So don't look back. You have already overcome. Now, survivor, move forward. It is what it is, you cannot change the past. Just learn from the past, forgive and keep going. Stay true to yourself and never cease to be authentic. Be the best you that you can be and make the future brighter. Live!

Don't worry about changing other people. That is God's job. You can only change yourself. Don't worry about what other people think. Concentrate on living in such a wondrous way that you are pleasing to God. He is the only One Whose opinion matters. Now, concentrate on making your goals realities. The more goals you accomplish, the sweeter your life and the more you can contribute to making a positive difference in others' lives.

Set your course. Focus on what is important, stick to your goals. Run your own race and stay in your lane. You must stay Positive. Let the past stay in the past.

If others have issues or negativity, that is their problem, so do not make it yours. Control what you can control: you, your thoughts and your actions by being proactive. Do not allow people to push your emotional triggers.

Say what you mean. Be concise as much as is possible. Think before you speak. Mean what you say.

Listen more, and speak less so you can really hear what others are saying. Herein is better communication.

Get active: it boosts creativity, heightens weight loss, promotes good health and gives restful sleep. A vigorous walk gets the heart pumping and clears the mind.

Be you, authentically genuine you, the gift you were divinely designed to be.

Count your blessings. Consider the positives more than the negatives, and you will realize how blessed you truly are.

Realize we each are a work in progress. God began the masterpiece that is you, and He is using life's situations to polish and develop the very best you that your life is designed to become. Look at yourself, your neighbor, your family member and see the face of God. Treat that person with dignity and respect, regardless of how they are treating you. Patience is developed among the sandpapery experiences, for like the oyster in the shell, the pearl within is only developed by constant sandy irritations to bring out its full luster. Painful process, certainly, for when people act like sandpaper, everything in me wants to scream, "Why me?" But it never was, and never will be about me. Life is about growth. Even if you have to stand alone, keep doing what it right, resting in the confidence that by living productively and proactively, you are glorifying God. Keep on making Him smile by doing your best, for it gives Him great pleasure.

Choose to look for the Nutella in life, the sweetness that will be amplified because living life flavorably will enable you to savor all the favor, beauty and enjoyment of the blessed life. Why look for Nutella? No, I am not talking about the scrumptious, decadent, chocolatey hazelnut spread that goes well with many creative culinary inspirations. By Nutella, I am speaking of living life with zest, passion and fulfillment, savoring the indescribably wonderful blessings and appreciating God's favor that enables you to be productive, positive and purposeful. It is of course a choice to be made, not unlike deciding to get up in the morning. We make choices all day, every day, so each of us is responsible for all decisions. So, instead of dwelling on vacuous, non-productive pursuits, look at where you are going in life. Decide to put your energy into that which makes life full of flavor and meaning. Whatever your passion is, live up to it, and be of help in the community while you have the opportunity.

"Long before he laid down earth's foundations, he had us in mind, and had settled on us as the focus of his love, to be made whole and holy by his love."
—Ephesians 1:4 NIV

51

BE A GARDENER:

Tend Your Garden by Making the Right Choices
to Improve the Quality of Daily Life

Everything begins with a choice, a selected idea of what direction you will take. Your choices make the difference, so choose wisely, for your greatest power is to choose.

Many people think gardening is something you only do where there is dirt. However, I realize that every day, we are planting seeds of ideas, mowing down weeds of unproductive ideas, tending our thought life which impacts our actions, and leading others either by positive or negative examples. May this book serve as a wise sage, guiding the reader through useful tips and tricks of the trade to improve your life. In short, the life we live is our garden, and we are the gardeners or farmers whose thoughts and choices can improve or destroy the quality of our own crops, and the crops of lives of others who are watching us. Our choices make the difference between fertile harvests and dismal defeat. Therefore, choose wisely, looking ahead at the road you are about to travel, and consider the reasons, benefits and disadvantages of why you are making that particular choice. The choices we make affect the type of lives we live.

In my reading and studies, I realize how vital it is for all of us in life, to be particularly diligent and vigilant about guarding our thoughts by controlling what enters our minds. You know that the word "vigilant" means to keep careful watch for possible danger or difficulties. This means we are to be hawk-eyed, be observant, attentive, stay on the lookout, eagle- eyed, keep on one's toes and be alert, taking every precaution to protect our mind from danger. It is often said that we are what we eat. Well, I would take that a step farther: we are what we think about.

For example, good health is critically important to me in mind, body and spirit. I realize that I am responsible for the degree of health that I have, for good health is wealth. That said, one of my recent choices is to be more active by exercising in a healthy, germ free environment, at least three times a week. Thusly, I really enjoy an invigorating walk outside. There are so many wonderful parks, hiking trails, lots of city wildlife and scenic places to enjoy. Looking at all the beautiful cloudscapes, sunshine, plants, lakes, birds, squirrels, butterflies and the occasional gopher, I swing my arms and behold the majesty of God's creation all around me. This is just what I need, fresh air, no contact with other people's sweat on gym equipment, no need for me to wait until I wipe down the selected equipment, just get up, get out and go walking. Only a pair of good walking shoes and comfortable clothing are needed to trek along whatever park or hiking trail once chooses, yet it wouldn't hurt to have a phone, a GPS, upbeat positive music and a pedometer with you as well. Also, it is always best to take safety precautions: take a walking buddy, if possible; be aware of your surroundings; choose an optimum daylight hour; choose a path where many people and security personnel are nearby; and look passersby in the eye so that you reduce the chance of sudden unpleasant surprises. With each step of my typical three mile trek, I breathe in the fresh air, thinking of all of the great blessings that have graced my life, and exhale more joyfully with each spoken or unspoken thought. For example, I found that there are so many things to be thankful for, that I stopped speaking them and just think about them, while giving thanks to Almighty God for each one. Thank You, Lord, for watching over me while I slept last night. You kept me safe from all sorts of dangers, seen and unseen. What a beautiful new day You have given me, straight from heaven's storehouse, full of great opportunities! Thank You for waking me up today, I'm so excited about all the ways You will show Your grace and mercy today. Thank You for each breath I am able to breathe! And look, Lord, no more wheezing, sniffling and sneezing, thank You for healing my many allergies! You healed my body, I have the mobility of each of my limbs. Thank You so much that I woke up in my right mind, full of purpose and strength. I'm so grateful for all the many ways that You are meeting needs not only in my life, but in the lives of people all around the world, answering prayers, encouraging hearts, giving hope. Thank You for using me to share a word of inspiration. May the gifts You've given me serve to help someone else have a better day and a joyful life full of purpose. Do you realize that the more gratitude you express, the more abundantly you enjoy life? I challenge each of us to take the time to inhale and exhale daily, realizing our blessings. Did you know that in Malachi 3:16-18, the New International Version, it says, *"Then those who feared the LORD talked with each other, and the LORD listened and heard. A scroll of remembrance was written in his presence concerning those who feared the LORD and honored his name. They will be mine, "says El Shaddai, "in the day when I make up my treasured possession. I will spare them just as in compassion a man spares his son who serves him. And you will again see the distinction between the righteous and the wicked; between those who serve God and those who do not."* Now, I like how the Amplified Version clarifies even further: "…those who reverenced and worshipfully feared the Lord and thought on His name." Wow! This is exciting! Do you realize that this is explaining that there is a book in heaven that is being written daily, recording every single time that we even think on or about His holy name? This is so powerful to see just how important our thoughts are! As we think about the goodness of God, meditating on His Word and how good He has been to each of us, God is making an eternal record in heaven of that. I'm sure that just like me, you reflect on the good things that have happened in your life. I think about how He saved me, strengthened me, delivered me from dangerous situations, brought me to the right people, gave me jobs, helped me find my way when life's difficulties came. He lifted me up when I was fallen, gave me joy when I was feeling down and out for the count. I think about all the times God made a way for me when there seemed to be no way. He has blessed me with His favor, His joy, His strength, His endurance and His presence. He gave me laughter and optimism and I know He has done as much for you because He is such a faithful God, full of mercy, grace and love. We live in such a negative world where people are more likely to say something bad rather than something good. Well, it takes the same amount of energy and breath. Let us each choose to make it a priority to speak life and gratitude. We are God's treasures, so let us exalt Him and choose to honor Him in our words. He is making an eternal record in a book that is ever before Him. It's not off in some back room, it's not up on a bookshelf somewhere gathering dust. No, the Book of Remembrance is right in front of Him, and every time we think about Him, study His Word, worship Him, pray and think on the things of God, He remembers us. He recalls each prayer, each time we worshipped Him, every time we encouraged one another or even just gave a hug to a brother in need. Let's choose to make the Book of Remembrance full, just overflowing with all the times we thought on the worthy name of God. What comfort it is to know that I have a Friend in my life, my heavenly Father, and I can depend on His help every step of this journey! I imagine the Lord is on His throne, asking the angel each time I'm reading His Word, praying and thanking Him, "Who is that you're writing about now? Well, God, I'm writing about (put your name here). She's/He's taking her/his walk in the park, just thanking You for all You've done. She/He just encouraged her/his friends and family, talking about Your faithfulness and how You'll work everything out for good." Imagine God smiling, joyful and happy, asking throughout the day what you and I did next that is pleasing to Him.

Now, along with having a grateful heart, instead of complaining as many do, I also challenge every one of us to carefully exercise diligence in our thought life. Remember, every action we take, every word we speak, every decision we make first comes through our minds. Each of us chooses what we think about, what we listen to, what we say, and what we do. That's the key: you and I choose. None of us were created to be robots. In fact, God designed each of us with the power to make choices. We each are responsible for our lives, so each of us must learn how to live life in the best way possible by guarding and controlling the thoughts we think. After all, I learned in Ephesians 6 that we each must *put on the full armor of God in order to be fully equipped to fight the battle of spiritual warfare we each are in.* Yes, we are in an all out battle every day. Yet God shares that *"My plans for you are good and not evil"* in Jeremiah 29:11 Amplified Bible:

[11] *For I know the thoughts and plans that I have for you, says the Lord, thoughts and plans for welfare and peace and not for evil, to give you hope in your final outcome.*

So, God planned the best for each of us, and according to John 10:10, *"The thief (the enemy) came only to steal and kill and destroy. I came that they may have and enjoy life, and have it in abundance (to the full, till it overflows)."* In order to experience this abundant life, we need to do what the doctor does, by giving ourselves a daily checkup, looking at what is keeping God's best blessings from flowing in our lives. As I reflect on my own life, and the lives of those who have confided in me, we all share the same root problem: our thinking was off balance, filled with anxiety, life's pressures, fear and defeat. We cannot listen to and think about negative thoughts, feelings and ideas and expect good to come from that. Conversely, we need to do what The Word says: *"...brethren, whatever is true, whatever is worthy of reverence and is honorable and seemly, whatever is just, whatever is pure, whatever is lovely and lovable, whatever is kind and winsome and gracious, if there is any virtue and excellence, if there is anything worthy of praise, think on and weigh and take account of these things [fix your minds on them]."* When I looked up the word winsome in the dictionary, I discovered this definition: "attractive or appealing in appearance or character; generally pleasing and engaging often because of a childlike charm and innocence <a **winsome** smile>; 2. cheerful, lighthearted." You see, living the victorious, overcoming joyful Christian life requires thinking about, talking about and actively using our will power to learn God's Word, apply it to our daily lives and resist the enemy in the name of Jesus Christ.

Now, the same people who want to whine, refusing to get some cheese to go with their whine, may say, "Well, I'm not a religious person. I don't believe in God. I'm busy with my family and career, on and on and on." We all can find excuses to do what we ought to do, yet all too easily we do what we should **not** do, then start complaining when things don't go our way. The reality is what you make a priority in your life, in other words, what you make important to you, is what becomes first in your life. None of us can expect to harbor hatred, bitterness, unforgiveness and let our minds be consumed with anxiety all day, every day, speaking negativity. Living that way results in a problem filled, miserable, negative and defeated life. As it is said, "garbage in, garbage out." It is necessary to have a focus and determination to make the change to live better. It's up to you and me, nobody else can do this for us. This is just like those who exercise: they get up, get out and get it done to make their health better, while watching what they eat and choosing to eat in moderation. For example, I walk at work as much as possible, then I walk to my parking space which often is a distance depending on my arrival time. Also, I don't eat everything my big eyes see and I certainly don't wolf down huge masses of food anymore. Now I eat in moderation. I pace myself. When my off button says, "Stop, that's enough," I stop. Why? I don't want to kill myself. I love myself, and there are people all around me who love me and whose lives are affected by what I do. So, in the same way, when something is important to each of us, we don't mind spending a little extra effort, extra energy and extra time on it because of the results we have in mind to reach our goal. So make it a top priority to control your thoughts, words and actions. It will please God. Also, not only will it be for your own good, but for the good of all those around you.

This reminds me of the 1960 Walt Disney movie, "Pollyanna." Both Hayley Mills, and in a later production, Keshia Knight Pulliam, provide stunning performances as the twelve-year old orphaned daughter of missionaries who arrives in the small town of Harrington to live with her rich aunt, Jane Wyman as Polly Harrington, around the 1900s. Pollyanna is a winsome, cheerful, radically optimistic youngster who focuses on the goodness of life and, in doing so, makes a wide variety of friends in the community including the hypochondriac Mrs. Snow, played by Agnes Moorehead, and the acidic recluse Mr. Pendergast, played by Adolphe Menjou.

Aunt Polly's wealth controls the town, and, when Harrington citizens want a derelict orphanage razed and rebuilt, Aunt Polly opposes the idea. The townspeople defy her by planning a carnival to raise funds for a new structure; however, because of the control Aunt Polly asserts over every facet of the town, numerous townspeople are reluctant to show their support. Aunt Polly is furious with their audacity and forbids Pollyanna to participate.

A group of citizens, led by Dr. Edmond Chilton attempt to persuade the town's minister, Reverend Ford to publicly declare his support for the bazaar by reminding him that "nobody owns a church." Reverend Ford is reminded of the truth of this statement while conversing with Pollyanna, who is delivering a note from Aunt Polly with recommendations about his sermon content.

At church the following Sunday, he declares his support for the bazaar and encourages all to attend, in defiance of Aunt Polly. On the evening of the carnival, Pollyanna is coaxed out of the house by playmate Jimmy Bean, who reminds her that she is leading "America, the Beautiful" at the high point of the event. With misgivings, she slips away and has a wonderful time at the carnival.

On returning home, she avoids Aunt Polly's presence by climbing a tree to her attic bedroom. When she reached her bedroom window, she falls and is severely injured, losing the use of her legs. Her spirits sink with the calamity, jeopardizing her chances of recovery. When Aunt

When Aunt Polly hears this, she feels saddened, realizes that she loves her niece very much, and feels a strong sense of guilt over Pollyanna's injuries, believing that it was her fault for not allowing Pollyanna to go to the carnival in the first place. When the townspeople learn of Pollyanna's accident, they gather *en masse* in Aunt Polly's house with outpourings of love. Pollyanna's spirits gradually return to their usual hopefulness and love of life. She departs Harrington with Aunt Polly for an operation in <u>Baltimore</u> that, it is hoped, will correct her injury. You see, Pollyanna's joyful optimism changed the folks in the community, whose perspectives changed by focusing on the good and choosing to make a positive difference.

Likewise, we too can turn things around in our lives and the lives of others. Let's start today!

Surely you have met or known an individual who, like Clark Kent, seemed quiet, shy, modest and ordinary, yet behind all of that was the most loving, gracious person you've ever met? Like any superhero, this person excels in exceptional talent and good works. However, he or she tends to be your typical unsung hero, rising to the occasion in a time of need. This unique person shines best in a trial's darkest hour and seasons of severe difficulties. Such a person is usually referred to as a diamond in the rough. Like naturally occurring diamonds, this incredible person may appear quite ordinary, perhaps even rough on the outside. Nonetheless, their true beauty and worth comes from the extreme pressure under which they are formed and the exceedingly harsh process of cutting and polishing that are used to reveal their inner beauty and value. Just as a cultured pearl is produced by the constant granular irritation of the sand within an oyster, life's difficulties help strengthen the Christian's faith as they also develop Godly character. Therefore, as I've often taught my students for over three decades, realize that you are a promise, alive to fulfill all the possibilities you were designed for. Here is a Bill Gaither song that I taught over the years to inspire my students. May the words encourage and inspire you.

I am a promise,
I am a possibility
I am a promise with a capital "P";
I can be anything, anything God wants me to be...

You are a promise!
You are a possibility!
You are a promise with a capital "P"!

Live Sunny Side Up!

You are a great big bundle of potentiality!
And if you'll listen, you'll hear God's voice;
And if you're trying, he'll help you make the right choices
You're a promise to be anything He wants you to be!

You can go anywhere that he wants you to go,
You can be anything that he wants you to be --
You can climb the high mountain,
You can cross the wide sea,
You're a great big promise you see!

I am a promise,
I am a possibility
I am a promise with a capital "P"!
I am a great big bundle of potentiality!
And I am learning to hear God's voice and I am tryin'
To make the right choices;
I'm a promise to be anything God wants me to be!

So keep on list'ning, you'll hear God's voice,
And keep on tryin', He'll help you make the right choices --
You're a promise to be anything He wants you to be!
I'm a promise to be anything God wants me to be!
You're a promise to be anything, anything He wants you to be!

BE HEALTHY:
LIKE OATMEAL, LIKE LIFE

And I will walk at liberty and at ease, for I have sought and inquired for, and desperately required, Your precepts. Psalm 119:45

Now the Lord is the Spirit, and where the Spirit of the Lord is, there is liberty (emancipation from bondage, freedom). 2 Corinthians 3:17

Life is like a delicious bowl of oatmeal. Not only is oatmeal good for you, but it is also as good as you choose to make it. You are in the driver's seat. Your thoughts and preferences determine how you will make the oatmeal. There are choices you have to make in order for it to be prepared. The specific flavor, whether maple and brown sugar, cinnamon and spice, apples and cinnamon, are all up to you. Also, the texture and added goodies are up to you. You can have fruit and cream, spice, raisins, caramel, slivered almonds, crushed walnuts, pecans or cashews, apple sauce, or Nutella. You can even choose to just have your oatmeal plain. Then the liquid is your choice entirely: you may choose 2% milk, almond milk, soy milk, or maybe even warm green tea or apple cider. How you make the oatmeal determines how healthy and enjoyable it will be.

Like oatmeal, God has given us the free choice or free will to make choices and decisions, preferably those that please Him. We should seek to please Him above everything else we can do. That goal should be our focus during each day we live on this earth. This mind set of desiring to please the Lord can protect us from being scatter brained, running all over the place, just throwing our energy to the winds. God gives us free will but that comes with a lot of personal responsibility.

Every day, we are presented with tons of choices. We firmly decide to do some things, and some decisions we just ignore, or don't make any decision at all. Now when that happens, we have already made a decision by default. There has to be a point of focus so that we have a guide to follow, or we will easily lose our way. This is why it is so important to stay in close prayerful communication with the Lord, for we live in His awesome presence and should be eternally grateful for all He does in our lives. We live in such a fallen world, full of far too many unexpected things that happen to unravel our live, get us off balance and distract our focus. A vibrant, thriving relationship with God can keep us from falling apart.

Colossians 3:23-24 *Whatever you do, work at it with all your heart, as working for the Lord, not for me, since you know that you will receive an inheritance from the Lord as a reward. It is the Lord Christ you are serving.*

What a wonderful life! There is power in changing your mindset towards Godliness and good health.

BE NOT ANXIOUS: WHY WORRY?

"Do not anticipate trouble, or worry about what may
never happen. Keep in the sunlight."

— Benjamin Franklin

This quote motivates me to refocus my attention on the light, the good, the positive, the beneficial and thereby redirect my energy to doing something productive. There is a scripture that shares, *"Be transformed by the renewing of your mind."* That is reminiscent of another verse that instructs me …*" If there be anything of good report, that is lovely, pure, praiseworthy….think on these things."*

It is all too easy to worry, to moan, to lament – as I began to do today when innocently retrieving my empty water bottle from the car during my work break. Just as I was about to return to my cubicle, I noticed something very odd on my rear car bumper, for the first time ever - several tiny to large scratches from the left end to the right end, looking as if some alien had etched some lengthy secret code there to identify my car to some unknown entity. A host of questions raced through my mind, as I tried to recall everywhere I'd been recently. Hmm, let's see: I went to the grocery store, the post office, home, work, church, relative's house, the mechanic's shop and the hairstylist. At none of those places had I noticed anything unusual. Then again, I seldom use the trunk of my car so it does not cross my mind to look back there until this particular moment. Was this the cause of a malicious person, or the scrawling of naughty, unattended children whose parents were not supervising them? Why would anyone do this to my car, which is usually parked in front of the garage, as close to the door as is possible? Whatever the reason, the tears welled up in my eyes.

I thought of what action items to put into play, since at work, when ideas come up, there is an action to bring it to fruition. My usual thing is to bottle up, keep it inside then implode. Today, I took a different approach, and talked about the concern, while seeking a solution from a wise, close friend who listened.

After deciding to speak about my concerns, first I called my best friend on my break, who is very wise, grounded and knowledgeable. After he listened to my possible causes and locations, I listened to his questions, then his final briefing was to help me find an inexpensive repair product that he'd seen before. Along with offering a great idea, his calming tone of voice really reduced my misery and helped me form a better perspective. First positive action! Next, I thought it best to make those welled up tears go away by talking to at least two more trusted colleagues at work. I made up my mind to take action. Of the next three people who allowed me to vent, one asked if it happened at work, which I could not prove, given this is a high security facility with cameras and no one except delivery people and the occasional dog walker are passing nearby, so no remedy there. The other two colleagues gave great remedies, one said, "Scratches are easy to repair, and understandably, now that you are more interested in cars, you are noticing more details like my girlfriend does." That's right, I reflected, I am noticing more instead of blindly going through the day as details pass me by. The next person offered the suggestion of clearing the garage, using shelves to store remaining items and thereby provide a place to park the car inside the garage to eliminate further concern. Overall, just talking and listening provided a sounding board that allowed me to make up my mind right then, and I thanked each of them and said, "OK, I'm just going to suck it up and get on with my work." No more tears, there is something to do that is productive. "Just stop it," I told myself, "and get on with it." I finished my tasks with gusto, and felt the burdensome load lift from my shoulders.

Now the funny part is that when I looked at the bumper, then looked at where I park, it was clearly noticed that the garage door handle is at the exact same height as the mysterious marks, and I rightly deduced that I had been parking too close to the garage door. How humbling and embarrassing! I felt about 2 inches tall, and resolved to park more cautiously. Obviously some physical body shop repairs will be done, but the greatest change needs to be made to correct my bad habit of parking hurriedly out of exhaustion. "Just take your time from now on," I told myself, "and do it right."

BE ACCOUNTABLE: REALIZE THAT TIME IS SUBLIME

Many years ago, I read C.S. Lewis' satirical 1942 book, "The Screwtape Letters." Both shocking and amusing, C S Lewis's satire The Screwtape Letters was a bestseller in its day, selling over half a million copies. It was a brilliant riposte to the creeping atheism, existentialism and materialism of Lewis's time, attracting the smart reader who normally may have dismissed Christianity as a moral guide; Lewis's Screwtape works relentlessly not simply to turn the victim towards sin, but to a fashionable resignation about the 'way of the world' that denies human progress.

The book is quite a challenge to understand, because everything is morally in reverse. You have to remind yourself that the 'Enemy' referred to is God, and that the way of life advocated by Screwtape is the exact opposite of a good Christian life. For instance, Screwtape bemoans that that the Enemy has given human beings free will to choose the Good, and that God actually loves 'the human vermin'.

Each chapter deals with a different temptation such as a lack of neighborly love, smugness, lust, and identifying with non-believers because they are clever and witty. Here is an excerpt from the book, which over the years has been deemed anonymous and changed by many on the Internet to fit the times we currently live in. I'm sure you will be amazed, as I was, at the incredibly on point statements. What follows is a brief synopsis of the book to put the excerpt in its proper context.

 Satan called a worldwide convention. In his opening address to his evil angels, he said, "We can't keep the Christians from going to church. We can't keep them from reading their Bibles and knowing the truth. We can't even keep them from conservative values. But we can do something else. We can keep them from forming an intimate, abiding relationship experience in Christ. If they gain that connection with Jesus, our power over them is broken. So let them go to church, let them have their conservative lifestyles, but steal their time, so they can't gain that experience in Jesus Christ. This is what I want you to do. Distract them from gaining hold of their Savior and maintaining that vital connection throughout their day!"

"How shall we do this?" shouted his angels.

"Keep them busy in the non-essentials of life and invent un-numbered schemes to occupy their minds," he answered.

"Tempt them to spend, spend, spend, then, borrow, borrow, borrow. Convince the wives to go to work for long hours and the husbands to work 6 or 7 days a week, 10-12 hours a day, so they can afford their lifestyles. Keep them from spending time with their children. As their family fragments, soon, their homes will offer no escape from the pressures of work."

"Over stimulate their minds so that they cannot hear that still small voice. Entice them to play the radio or cassette player whenever they drive, to keep the TV, VCR, CDs and keep PCs going constantly in their homes. Keep them so busy with their electronic devices that they fail to reflect on God's Word. Entice them with too much information so that their minds will be dizzy and unable to focus on having an intimate relationship with their Savior and Lord. And see to it that every store and restaurant in the world plays non-biblical music constantly. This will jam their minds and break that union with Christ."

"Fill their coffee tables with magazines and newspapers. Pound their minds with the news 24 hours a day. Invade their driving moments with billboards. Flood their mailboxes with junk mail, sweepstakes, mail order catalogs, and every kind of newsletter and promotional offering, free products, services, and false hopes."

"Give them Santa Claus to distract them from teaching their children the real meaning of Christmas. Give them a Thanksgiving turkey so they will forget to give thanks for salvation through Jesus Christ. Give them an Easter bunny so they won't talk about His resurrection and power over sin and death. Even in their recreation, let them be excessive. Have them return from their recreation exhausted, disquieted and unprepared for the coming week. Don't let them go out in nature to reflect on God's wonders. Send them to amusement parks, sporting events, concerts and movies instead. And when they meet for spiritual fellowship, involve them in gossip and small talk so that they leave with troubled consciences and unsettled emotion."

"Let them be involved in soul-winning. But crowd their lives with so many good causes they have no time to seek power from Christ. Soon they will be working in their own strength, sacrificing their health and family unity for the good of the cause."

It was quite a convention in the end. And the evil angels went eagerly to their assignments causing Christians everywhere to get busy, busy, and busy, rushing here and there.

Do you sense the busyness of the world today? I know I do. This story so accurately portrays the temptations Satan uses to keep us from developing an intimate connection with Jesus. Yet as I look back over God's leading in my life, purpose and family, I have found God's Word to be true: *"In your presence is fullness of joy; At your right hand are pleasures forever more,"* Psalms 16:11, NKJV.

Look at your life. I guess the question is: has the devil been successful at his scheme? You be the judge. Take heed of the message you just read and remember:

B =Being

U =Under

S =Satan's

Y =Yoke

Screwtape is a senior devil whose job is to increase the store of malice and misery on Earth. He achieves this by carefully targeting humans and then providing them with an array of temptations that can take their minds away from God.

Under Screwtape's charge is his nephew Wormwood, a novice devil. The letters between them record their efforts to turn a young man from his newly-adopted Christianity back to 'Our Father Below' (Satan). Wormwood receives detailed instructions on how to exploit the man's weaknesses and bring him permanently around to sin.

Both shocking and amusing, C S Lewis's satire, The Screwtape Letters, was a bestseller in its day, selling over half a million copies. It was a brilliant riposte to the creeping atheism, existentialism and materialism of Lewis's time, attracting the smart reader who normally may have dismissed Christianity as a moral guide; Lewis's Screwtape works relentlessly not simply to turn the victim towards sin, but to a fashionable resignation about the 'way of the world' that denies human progress.

The book is quite a challenge to understand, because everything is morally in reverse. You have to remind yourself that the 'Enemy' referred to is God, and that the way of life advocated by Screwtape is the exact opposite of a good Christian life. For instance, Screwtape bemoans that that the Enemy has given human beings free will to choose the Good, and that God actually loves 'the human vermin'.

Each chapter deals with a different temptation such as a lack of neighborly love, smugness, lust, and identifying with non-believers because they are clever and witty.

Beginning the assault

We are made aware that Screwtape and Wormwood's victim is an eligible bachelor, and they work on getting him hitched to various unsavory women. They are horrified when their man falls in love with a Christian woman of good repute and family. At this point they realize

69

it is no use trying to turn him away from his growing spirituality, so instead attempt to corrupt what spiritual feeling he does have. As the victim moves in intellectual Christian circles, they make him attracted to fashionable ideas, such as: the church is a mere bureaucratic perversion of the original intention of its founder; Jesus is a mere historical figure and not really divine; and Christianity on its own is not enough; one has to ally it to social programs to 'create a better society'. The idea is to make him feel that Christianity on its own is a little old-hat, that to make it really come alive in the greater population is must be made sexier.

This ploy works. The victim is now moving in a fast set of intellectuals far in advance of him, and Screwtape succeeds in instilling in the man a certain spiritual pride. The idea is to make him feel that as a Christian he is better than others, and as an intellectual Christian he is even more special. Screwtape tells Wormwood: "The idea of belonging to an inner ring, of being in a secret, is very sweet to him. Play on that nerve. Teach him...to adopt an air of amusement at the things the unbelievers say."

We'll get him still

The book is set in wartime England when bombs threaten to rain down and kill. Wormwood is excited at this prospect, but Screwtape tells him not to be so silly: it is better that their victim be kept alive. Why? Because if he survives the bombs they will have him in the palm of their hand, because with the advancing years he will succumb to the spiritual wasteland of middle age. Routine and the failure of youthful hopes and loves, they are sure, will turn him their way. Screwtape gleefully writes of "the drabness which we create in their lives and the inarticulate resentment with which we teach them to respond to it: all this provides admirable opportunities of wearing out a soul by attrition."

However, if the man is successful and prosperous, Screwtape slyly observes, "our position is even stronger". He explains that prosperity cements a person to worldly concerns by increasing their place in it. If they become well known and important with many connections, what need will they have of God? The goal of the dark side is to increase attachment to the earthly concerns, and this becomes easier with age. In contrast, the spontaneity and love of life of the young (or young at heart) makes it very difficult for him and his kind to win a human over to their side.

The final assault

Screwtape's larger aim is to prevent the victim from gaining any self-knowledge. The idea is to keep him locked into raw emotions which cancel out any hope for objectivity and reflection. As the bombs fall on London, Wormwood suggests injecting a bit of cowardice into the man, but Screwtape says 'No!' - cowardice brings on shame, which can lead to self-evaluation and a desire to be a stronger person.

The diabolical two try to get the victim to not persevere in anything, to fail in his resolutions, to not make commitments, as all such things make a person evolve into something better. They want him to feel that he is the master of his destiny who does not need God's help. In times of adversity, Screwtape observes, "the fun is to make the man yield just when (had he but known it) relief was almost in sight."

When the man sees burning flesh on the wall of a bombed-out house, the devils hope they have succeeded in making him believe that life is just a house of horrors with no meaning. But the man shocks them by seeing beyond the rubble to the miracle of life. He is now well beyond the reach of the devil. Screwtape had described the victim as: "This animal, this thing begotten in a bed." Now that same animal sees in the same way that God does.

Final word

When Lewis wrote The Screwtape Letters his writing was already known to a huge audience who had listened to his 'Ten Minute Talks' on the BBC in the early years of the Second World War. These talks covered his conversion to Christianity, morality and many other subjects. The book was dedicated to his friend JRR Tolkien.

The Screwtape Letters may have seemed to represent what was going on in the political world, but the author's real concern was the inner life and the decisions we make every day. The old-fashioned morality that the book espouses still packs a punch, and although Lewis wrote as a Christian, the reader can easily substitute their own devils for his Screwtape and Wormwood.

Is painting the world in terms of 'good and evil' too simplistic? Perhaps, but Lewis's quirky presentation of the polarities as real is quite convincing and makes you think about all the rationalizations we make to justify our thoughts and actions. What we can take from this book is a reassurance that there is something in us that is naturally resistant to corruption - and that by being true to ourselves we can succeed in increasing that resistance.

Be confident in God.

I am the Door; anyone who enters in through Me will be saved (will live). He will come in and he will go out (freely), and will find pasture. John 10:9

Lean on, trust in, and be confident in the Lord with all your heart and mind and do not rely on your own insight or understanding. In all your ways, acknowledge Him and He will make straight your paths. Proverbs 3:5-6

Be quick to forgive. *Bear with each other and forgive whatever grievances you may have against one another. Forgive as the Lord forgave you.* Colossians 3:13

Be outrageously blessed. *Delight yourself also in the Lord, and He will give you the desires and secret petitions of your heart.* Psalm 37:4

Be content. *...for I have learned how to be content (satisfied to the point where I am not disturbed or disquieted) in whatever state I am in.* Philippians 4:11

Be a Bee Keeper: Keep On Keeping On

This first poem is meant to inspire any one of us. It talks about being strong enough to pick ourselves up during difficult times.

See setbacks as opportunities for growth. If we learn to get through the tough times, and embrace failure, there's nothing that will stop us from achieving our dreams, whatever they may be.

Life is beautiful. If we decide to live our lives with a positive attitude, then life will be so much more enjoyable. Our eyes and hearts will also be open to opportunities.

Here are three inspirational poems that speak about life and faith. May they remind us that life never travels down a straight or smooth path. There will always be difficulties and obstacles to work through. We need to learn from these bumps in the road that we can overcome by faith in God. By learning this, we will be better prepared for our journey ahead.

Give It Our All

Never ever give in,

to complaints nor fear.

With our eyes on our goals,

the right direction we'll steer.

No matter how tough the situation,

with great effort we should try.

We must pick ourselves up,

when we fall, get bruised and cry.

Opportunities are plentiful,

let us open our eyes.

Our dreams we shall nurture,

as we trust God from on high.

Let us seek to find value,

that is honest and real.

By faith and purpose,

we'll gain that victory surreal.

If we never hold back,

and just give it our all.

No challenge or obstacle,

shall ever be too tall.

-Vicki Evans

Passion for Life

The path in your life

may not often be straight

So full of bumps and curves

Some turned back though deemed great.

Your personal experiences

have shaped who you are.

Embrace all your mistakes

and each unique scar.

There are always new things

in life that we may learn.

With every new page,

with each chapter we turn.

There is only one simple

yet vitally important rule.

Your passion for life

must be used as your fuel.

-Vicki Evans

Sincerely, I think it is critically important for each of us to live life based on our faith, integrity and values. In doing this, we are less likely to be fighting against the grain, and things will fall into place by divine design in God's fullness of time, as we do our part by living obediently.

Let us set our minds, let faith in God lead us, pursue our goals passionately and conduct ourselves with integrity and dignity as we choose to live intelligently. Now, take courage and be strong, fortified by these next words.

"Be strong in the Lord and in His mighty power."

—Ephesians 6:10

Be strong in the Lord and be of good courage, your mighty Commander will vanquish the foe. Fear not the battle for the victory is His. He will protect you wherever you go.

—LL Johnson

Lord, we pray not for tranquility nor that our tribulations may cease. We pray for Your Spirit and Your love, that You grant us strength and grace to overcome adversity through Jesus Christ our Lord. Amen.

—Girolamo Savonarola, 15th Century

"...For God did not give us a spirit of cowardice, but rather a spirit of power and of love and of self discipline."

—2 Timothy 1:7

"You then, my child, be strong in the grace that is in Christ Jesus; and the things you have heard me say in the presence of many witnesses entrust to reliable men who will also be qualified to teach others. Endure hardship with use like a good soldier of Christ Jesus. No one serving as a soldier gets involved in civilian affairs: he wants to please his Commanding Officer.

Here is a trustworthy saying: If we died with Him, we will also live with Him; If we endure, we will also reign with Him; If we disown Him, He will also disown us; If we are faithless, He will remain faithful, for He cannot disown Himself. Do your best to present yourself to God as one approved, a workman who does not need to be ashamed and who correctly handles the Word of Truth." —2 Timothy 1:1-4, 11-13, 15 NIV

BE PREPARED WITH THE FULL ARMOR OF GOD

"Finally, be strong in the Lord and in His mighty power. Put on the full armor of God so that you can take your stand against the devil's schemes. For our struggle is not against flesh and blood, but against the rulers, against the authorities, against the powers of this dark world and against the spiritual forces of evil in the heavenly realms.

Therefore put on the full armor of God, so that when the day of evil comes, you may be able to stand your ground, and after you have done everything, to stand. Stand firm then, with the belt of truth buckled around your waist, with the breastplate of righteousness in place, and with your feet fitted with the readiness that comes from the gospel of peace.

In addition to all this, take up the shield of faith, with which you can extinguish all the flaming arrows of the evil one. Take the helmet of salvation and the sword of the Spirit, which is the Word of God. And pray in the [Holy] Spirit on all occasions with all kinds of prayers and requests. With this in mind, be alert and always keep on praying for all the saints." —Ephesians 6:10-18

Teach us, good Lord, to serve You as You deserve; to give and not to count the cost; to fight and not to heed the wounds; to toil and not to seek for rest; to labor and not to ask for any reward, except that of knowing that we do Your will, through Jesus Christ our Lord, Amen. – Ignatius of Loyola, 16th Century

Be An Overcomer: Weathering the Storms of Life

Whatever the weather report may reveal, I rejoice to be invigorated by the cool breezes, the warmth of the sun, the mists of the rain and the icy freshness of snow. Yet of all weather conditions, I particularly enjoy the rain showers that water the plants and cleanse the soot and grime from pollution, leaving behind a delightfully fragrant and moist environment. The best part of the showers is being inside, warm and dry, enjoying a steaming hot cup of tea or hot chocolate, while watching the beauty unfold through the windows.

As in the weather, also in life's journey, sometimes the rain and thunderstorms come our way. As the dark clouds blanket the sky, I am often reminded of a painting lesson learned long ago. I was working on my ability to showcase light in one of my painting projects. Taking a tour of a friend's home, I encountered a print of one of Claude Monet's impressionist paintings, entitled "The Water Garden at Giverny." Although the original full scale work is in a Paris museum, I was still enthralled by the luxuriant water garden due to its delightful array of colors. As I looked closer, I was surprised to notice the stark contrast between the delicately painted pastel flowers and the striking deep hues of the water garden. In fact, the major part of the canvas seems covered by the darker colors which actually highlight the exquisitely rich florals of the water lilies. The amazing contrast draws my eyes first to the lovely colorful petals until I realize that it is the darker tones that enhance their presence, much like the dark shadows of nearby objects are noticed in the presence of light.

This painting reminds me of my life and my Heavenly Father's artistry, Who designed me with a purpose and design. Truly, life's storms cause me to focus all too often on the darkness in my life's journey, yet it through my Lord's artistry that the black, gray, blue and other dark hues in my life painting are put to good use, brushed onto my life canvas for a greater purpose, to make my life richer and more meaningful in its impact on me and those with whom I am brought into contact. Through the difficulties, disappointments and challenges, and the expectations that were dashed into pieces, God's handiwork creates a brilliant palette of beauty and color from my experiences of suffering, pain and trials. The Artist's multitude of techniques weave our experiences to develop us into the people we were created to be. Just like these masterfully painted water lilies, Father God uses the rainsoaked, stormy trials of life to shape us like a potter shapes the clay into a beautifully crafted work of art. Through it all, He keeps us afloat by His grace, mercy and love to thrive by His help. May this encourage and strengthen us all, for this storm will pass and leave us better. That reminds me of an encouraging letter sent to me years ago by a dear friend, from which I share an excerpt below:

In this vision, I arrived in Heaven, and I was standing in a long queue to face the Lord. Around me were other people carrying gifts, beautifully wrapped and carefully carried to prevent damage. Each person was careful to have their gift ready for when their name was called. I looked at my empty hands, and wondered what was happening. I did not understand why I did not have a gift everyone else seemed to. It was not as if they collected their gifts from somewhere, and it was not as if they arrived with them. Their gifts seemed to be part of each one of them and one with them.

I asked a few of them about their gifts, to try and understand what was different about me, but the answers were all the same. "We are sorry. We do not know about you. These gifts are the works we have accomplished for our Lord. They are the projects we did, the plans we had for our lives that we brought to fruition as Christians. This is what we are offering to the Lord we have waited our whole lives for this. We do not understand what the reason could be that you do not have such a gift for the Lord."

I became insecure in this and feared the Judgment of the Lord. All I could imagine was standing before the Throne of Grace, without a gift, and being singled out by the Lord as the only one not bearing a gift. As far as I could see I was the only one who had no gift.

Before I knew it, my name had been called, and I walked slowly towards the Throne of the Lord. It was not that I feared Him not in that way, anyway, but I was imagining me stepping up to the Judgment seat and saying to God "I am sorry all these others have brought You gifts, big and small, and there has been such ceremony each time. Their life s work is before You and You have been pleased with it, I have no such gift to offer You. I do not have a significant thing that I have achieved which consumed me my whole life." He rose from His seat, smiled and said "Do not trouble yourself about offering Me a gift today. Come with me I have something to show you. I have been waiting, looking forward to the time when you will come before me. I received from you every day that you walked with Me, and I have kept these things, to show you." Then He took me to a room, the four walls of which contained a magnificent tapestry. As I looked at it, I saw familiar scenes and details from my life but not so much MY life being illustrated, as the lives of others and the Kingdom of God, where their lives and purposes have touched mine. At every point where my life and someone else's life touched, there began two golden threads the one leading from my life into theirs, and the other leading from their life into mine. God looked at this Tapestry with deep affection, and began to trace the golden threads with His finger. Each single thread, one by one, was traced from the start of each single thread to the end of each individual, unique thread.

As I watched His finger, and looked at the expression on His face, I began to see the effect of the Golden threads on the tapestry. I saw how they brightened certain sections that would have been very dark otherwise; how they drew together sometimes two, sometimes more sections with a complexity and intricacy of design that left me astounded; how in certain places they formed a basket of sorts, a supportive structure that framed and held a scene from another's life; sometimes the threads seemed to form a path between areas of the tapestry a path that enabled a flow and a progression from one scene to another with no chance of going astray.

After a long while, He turned to me and said "Do you see? Each golden thread you see before you, is an act of obedience done by you. Sometimes your obedience was in the form of acting, speaking or interceding in another's life. Sometimes that obedience was your ear, attuned for My voice, and your hearing and doing what I asked. Sometimes it was others' voices, or My own voice, that you chose to hear and in humility, allowed My Holy Spirit to change you.

I know you could not possibly have seen this from your time on earth. This tapestry has been woven joyfully in secret, by my angels, who have watched and celebrated your life and your obedience to me. This has been a lifetimes work your lifetime, their joyful work. They stand in this audience behind you, honored to have woven this for you. You sent them such volumes and quality of material, that their work was easy. This tapestry has been made for this day, this time, and this place. It is now revealed, divinely designed to be your unique gift to Me.

These golden threads were your gift to Me every day of your life.

This tapestry is the sum total of your gift to Me. You do not stand before Me empty handed, my little one. You stand before Me obedient, day by day, opportunity by opportunity, and the gift to Me that that obedience is, is so huge that you could not have carried it into My presence even if you had been aware of what it was. It is also more complicated and intricate than human hands could have woven. The beauty of a life poured out as a daily offering, and the beauty of a love expressed through the obedience that is detailed and remembered for all time here before Us, could not have been crafted by human hands. It is beyond mere human ability to do this work."

Somehow, in listening to Him, I had not seen the room change, and while the tapestry remained, it was as if there were no longer walls. We were back before the Throne of Grace, and the Words He spoke were no longer a gentle conversation. They were His Judgment over my life. As with each life that had gone before me, Heaven broke into thunderous applause at the Judgment, and as I walked away from the Throne to the place reserved for me, I began to realize that my steps were taking me past and into a gallery of people who were familiar beyond all expectation. As I saw their faces, I saw reflected in them the golden threads that I had sowed in their life, and began to see in myself, the threads that they had sown in my life. These people were my inheritance. I was awed at the richness of it all.

Chapter Epilogue

The Mourning After

Far be it from me to discuss living on the sunny side of life without acknowledging one of the most difficult experiences of all, the death of a loved one. In the Christian community, this is referred to as the homegoing, for as the Bible enlightens us, "absent from the body, present with the Lord." I listened to some bereaved people sharing their heartfelt concerns on the news and felt it best to try to paraphrase their wisdom, in the hopes of encouraging anyone who has suffered a loss.

To some, these are most helpful while mourning:

- ❖ Seeing and hearing the loved one's name or photo

- ❖ Sharing a familiar memory of the dearly departed

- ❖ Reference to those remaining as the loved one's relative or friend

- ❖ Use of the relationship with loved ones in present tense

- ❖ Acknowledging the life and contributions of the loved one

- ❖ Recognizing that the grieving may last long after the homegoing service

- ❖ Remembering the loved one, as some said: "his/her spirit is still here"

- ❖ Realizing that those who remain may not get over the passing, as little things (music, aromas, favorite items, and special days like holidays, birthdays, Christmas, Fathers' Day or Mothers' Day) may remind them of their beloved

- ❖ Understanding, prayer, patience, scriptures, comfort, hugs, tissues and compassion

- ❖ Caring expression, voice mails and gestures showing that you care

- ❖ Music, cards, poetry and artistic expressions that inspire and speak to the heart

- ❖ Thoughtful, practical gifts; easy to reheat meals, comfort food, groceries or a shopping gift certificate, house cleaning services, home organizing, babysitting, pet sitting or a spa day gift certificate

- ❖ Space and time to overcome without pressure to attend events

❖ Books and blogs like the link to Glow in the Woods, which features expressive, soulful guest writers (www. glowinthewoods.com) from which this brief poetic excerpt comes:

"There is the moment before…

A candle, a warm glow, a dancing spit of light

And there is after.

I learn the word fire…the word burn.

The world will never be the same…

You sit, embedded in my chest,

Irretrievable,

A bright, hard bead."

BE RICH: THE BEST OF ALL RICHES

Image can be changed overnight, yet character takes a lifetime to develop.

Choose a good reputation over great riches; being held in high esteem is better than silver or gold. - Proverbs 22:1 NLT

*A **good** name is to be more desired **than** great **wealth**, Favor is **better than** silver and gold. - Proverbs 22:1 KJV*

A good reputation is built on good character not a false image.

If you have character, you have the better part of wealth.

After observing the often catastrophic daily news and the frequently egregious media programming over a period of time, it is my firm conviction that it is time to do something about restoring good character, high ethics and consistent integrity to our lives, media and way of thinking. Too often, our society seems drawn by blood lust by the media's usual focus on something negative in their programming: infidelity, a person's shoddy image, criminal tendencies, arguments, fighting, anger, hostilities, lies, bad character, or a lack of integrity in business, politics or just in daily life. I understand that ratings are important, and there are some programs that are partially enjoyable for the short term, yet overall, I prefer wholesome programming and literature with a powerfully positive message, and biographies of those who overcame against all odds, or helped the underdogs they encountered in their businesses or daily lives. That feeds my inspirations, hopes and aspirations, filtering into my teaching repertoire. As a matter of fact, sometime during my three decades of teaching, I came across a memorable story somewhere from literature written by John Griggs as I was teaching a standards based thematic unit to my students about courage and character. Allow me to share what I recall of the heartwarming story, "The Night We Won the Buick."

A young boy was ashamed because his poor family was the only one in town that did not own a car. His mother used to advise him "if you have character, you have the better part of wealth." However, the boy wondered what use having character was if it could not buy a car. Then an opportunity came in the form of a country fair in which a new Buick Roadmaster was going to be raffled off. The boy's father's name was announced as the winner. The boy was elated to see his dream come true. This brand new car was theirs! However, he found his parents deeply engaged in an ethical debate. His mother explained the dilemma. Father had bought two raffle tickets, one for himself and another one for his boss. He had marked the name of his boss on one of the ticket stubs. The ticket that won the car actually belonged to his boss, so the car did not belong to his father. However, the boss did not know the number of his ticket. The boy felt there was no need to inform the boss about it for the boss was extremely rich. The boss already owned a fleet of cars and there was no way he was ever going to know that it was his ticket that won the car. However, the father phoned his boss and asked him to take the car. The family could not afford to buy a car for several years more and the boy grew up. As time went on, his mother's aphorism, " if you have character, you have the better part of wealth" took a new meaning for him. Looking back, he realized that they were never richer than they were at that moment, when his father made that telephone call, and returned the car to his boss. His father chose to do the right thing instead of yielding to the temptation of dishonesty.

The fact that this refreshing story by John Grigg is included in school books makes me particularly grateful in this age of often demonstrated self indulgence, immediate gratification and a lack of integrity, doing whatever is considered necessary to win at any cost. John's Grigg's story provides a life-long lesson on integrity, in that it shows that the father could have kept that new car. Instead, he decided to return it to its rightful owner. How many times do we see such a display of integrity? In my humble opinion, it is critically important to model and teach lessons in character and integrity to children and impressionable young adults. Therefore, it behooves all adults to realize that now is the time that we all should model these priceless attributes in our daily behavior and focus on imparting practical lessons in integrity, daily ethics and character development. In this world of instant information by way of global media and technological advances, this includes those in the neighborhoods and the media, whether firefighters, business owners, police officers, paramedics, preachers, rabbis, neighbors, teachers, news broadcasters, talk show hosts, actors, famous sports figures or politicians, along with a host of others who are seen and heard, whether they feel responsible or not. The reality is that anyone that is visible, audible or read about to impressionable children and young adults can and does influence how their lives are shaped. What we think, say and do exponentially impacts the world around us. Let's choose to make a positive impact.

As I've often said to the parents of my students, parents are the first teachers, and I am privileged to be a support member of the team, for it all begins in the home. While training new teachers, I have emphasized curricular development, lesson planning and classroom management, in addition to the critical role that parents play in laying a firm foundation of core values in their children. Parents, relatives, friends and other supportive adults need to be the role models for children. Their actions talk best. Getting involved in children's thinking and activities holds the key and provides opportunities to parents to lay a strong foundation: brick-by-brick. We have all come across situations like these:

While children are playing baseball, soccer or football, the ball unfortunately hits a neighbor's house or car window and breaks the glass. Now, the parents could ignore what happened by thinking it is not only their child who did it, but others who are guilty as well. Conversely, the parents could take responsibility for what happened by taking their child over to the neighbor's house to apologize and offer to pay whatever it costs to get the glass replaced. This simple act teaches the child some vitally important lessons:

- ❖ *Be honest about what happened.*

- ❖ *Accept responsibility for your actions.*

- ❖ *Apologize when your actions have caused inconvenience or harm to someone.*

- ❖ *Demonstrate what it means to be a good neighbor.*

Children are generally excited in their moments of successes. Parents and other responsible, interested adults who are present, need to make it a priority to be with them in such teachable moments, for it is essential to discuss with children how they achieved their success. This is an opportunity for the child to explain what he or she did and why they did it. When there is an open, honest and friendly communication, the child may confide in them that, for example, the basketball referee did not notice when the child pushed the opposing team's player, causing that person to miss making the shot, which caused the child to make the winning shot, and they won the game. Now, we have an opportunity to impart another lesson of integrity: ***how you achieve something is more important that what you achieve.*** We can explore the options of correcting such a mistake like accepting it in front of the referee or other team, apologizing, or even returning the trophy. If the child does any of these, it is vital that parents and others present show their instant appreciation in words and actions.

Also, the moments of failures provide rich opportunities that must not be missed in a child's character development. Parents often make the mistake of burdening the children with huge expectations. This puts them under a lot of stress. Some children even take the ultimate step and commit suicide if they don't achieve the desired result. What is the big deal if they do not get above 90 %, or if they do not get selected in a contest, or win in a sport? That does not lessen their value as a person who chose to participate and did their best. We all need to acknowledge the effort put in by the child. It is a good idea to celebrate the effort of the child by taking him/her out for dinner or to a movie. The child feels good and is encouraged to try harder the next time and learns important lessons: *put in your best effort and don't worry about the result; there is always a next time; and even if you don't achieve what you are aiming for, it is not the end of the world… there are more opportunities to explore.*

There may be many more examples of actions that parents can take. Each action is like laying a brick in foundation of building character of our children. If the initial bricks are not laid properly, the building may not be strong.

We live in a world that is increasingly more focused on bad character, dishonesty and the lack of integrity. However, character and obedience always matter first to God. Matthew 1:19, New King James Version says, "Joseph, Mary's husband, was a just man…" Although seldom noticed and seldom appreciated in many recreations of the Christmas drama, God chose Joseph just as carefully as He chose Mary. The Bible says that God saw that Joseph was a just man. Now that is quite a tribute from Almighty God. He may have chosen Joseph to model spiritual devotion for Jesus, for Joseph's character, priorities, example, lifestyle and personal faith surely would be extremely influential in the Jesus' earliest years. God knew Joseph would face a difficult choice, as recorded in Matthew 1:18-25, and God knew that he would make a just and righteous decision. Joseph could protect his good name by choosing not to marry Mary, who was divinely pregnant, or he could choose to provide a home for Mary and this miracle child. He could not do both. Life gives you choices to make but not all of the possible options are equal.

Mary would certainly need a just man to accept her as is and protect her in this vulnerable state, someone to stand firmly between her and the predictable whispers of the disapproving friends, and perhaps even her family. The young Jesus would need a just father to teach Him the ways of God. So God chose Joseph, who was a just and righteous man. Character and obedience always matter first to

God. That is a lifelong truth. When God has something important to be done, He always chooses those who consistently put God first. Just imagine the grand plans God has for your life when you choose to put Him first! Joseph had history with God. God could trust his choices. Let us choose to do God's will first and foremost, then God will put everything else in its proper place. You choose to put first or in first priority whoever or whatever you consider to be of first importance. Jesus put the Father first because the Father was His priority. Jesus also modeled this priority by saying in John 8:29 NKJV, *"I always do those things that please the Father."* In each of our lives, we have the opportunity to live more justly and sacrificially every single day, in everysingle way. Let us choose to live in such a way that our history with God allows fulfillment of our destiny in God.

I remember a story that I read a long time ago to my students, that I believe is written by Alexandra Ruskin. In my many teaching notes I found a snippet of the story. This interesting story was about a child talking about his father's childhood dreams. Here is an excerpt: When my father was a child, he was often asked what you would like to be when you grew up. He had different answers each time. First he said he would become a night watchman so that he could roam around freely when everyone else was asleep. Next, he wanted to be an ice cream vendor: have as much ice cream as you want, yet be able to roam around. Later, he aspired to become a railway engine driver. His parents would laugh at his answers. Father's dreams kept on changing with time, from becoming a pilot, to becoming an actor and so on. Finally, he said he wanted to become a dog. As a dog he could run fast on four legs, bark at people, run after them and laze around, all at his will. He had one problem though. He was unable to scratch his back with his leg like dogs do. He started spending time with dogs to learn the trick. One day an army officer passed by and asked him, "What are you doing with dogs?" Father replied, "I am learning how to be a dog." When the officer asked why, the father said, "I have been a human for some time and now I want a change."

The officer asked him, "Do you know what a human being is?" The father said "No" and asked him to explain. The officer said, "Think about it" and left. Father kept on thinking and realized that he must first learn to become a good human being. This time when he shared his desire with his parents, no one laughed. Father had finally learned his life lesson: Be a good human being.

We occasionally hear it said about someone, "He is out to make a name for himself." We understand that statement to mean that he is seeking notoriety or fame. A big name or a famous name is not necessarily a good name. While teaching a careers unit, I asked my students what they wanted to be, and I heard a variety of answers. Most children wanted positions that earned large amounts of money and fame. Only a few students said they wanted to be good human beings and help others, and that included helping their families and communities. I clarified that being a good human being also means having a good name, a good reputation and good character, concepts which we explored further with concrete examples, discussions, activities and culminating projects. When I asked about why the students chose their responses, I was told that times were hard and money was needed more than anything else. Others said that they wanted to be famous like those they had seen on TV. Many students changed their answers after hearing those who chose to be good human beings, for as one student stated after sharing the downfall of a sports figure, "Money comes and goes, but being good is forever." What wisdom from one so young! This led to my sharing with the class that having a good name is a genuine asset or treasure that must be valued. One should guard his reputation against whatever might ruin it. A good past makes an excellent future reference. We pursued this concept over the course of the unit and surmised the following conclusions:

There are several reasons why a good reputation is to be chosen in preference to riches.

(1) A good name will secure what money cannot buy. Some who are loaded with wealth have a bad name, and no amount of money can purchase a good reputation for them. People trust someone who has a good name. The accumulation of wealth does not make one more trustworthy.

(2) A good name has a higher quality than material wealth. Riches may bring someone great fame, but there is a difference between great fame and a good name. Additionally, in my Sunday School class, I shared that a good name is "a name for good things with God and good people" as quoted by Matthew Henry.

(3) A good name enables one to do more good than riches without a good name can do. A good reputation opens doors of opportunity. Respect and esteem are worth far more than silver and gold.

For example, Abraham had a good name **and** great riches because God honored His promise to him, "I will bless thee, and make thy name great" in Genesis 12:2. Also, the Bible describes Abraham as being "very rich in cattle, in silver, and in gold" in Genesis 13:2. In reviewing Proverbs 22:1, "A good name is to be more desired than great wealth, Favor is better than silver and gold," the point of our proverb is that if one must choose between a good reputation and riches, the former should be chosen. Moffatt translates Proverbs 22:1 as: "Reputation is a better choice than riches; esteem is more than money." To have a good name is to possess a good reputation. The name which one earns for himself through righteous deeds is far more important than the name on his birth certificate. It is said of Jesus during His youthful years, "And Jesus increased in wisdom and stature and in favor with God and man" according to Luke 2:52. What a contrast that is with some people today who do not care at all about being in good standing with neither God or man!

Now, in both classes, I taught that reputation refers to one's overall qualities as judged by people in general, or in other words, how other people see you and what opinion they have of you. Of course, people often err in their estimation of others. It seems likely that the proverb is referring to a good name as one is judged in the eyes of others who are good and righteous people.

On the other hand, character refers to the sum of distinctive qualities belonging to an individual. One's reputation is not always a true measure of his character. However, a good name that is based on good character brings goodwill and admiration from all who value goodness. Both character and reputation are important. Every child of God must endeavor to develop the best qualities of character. He or she should try to keep a good name.

Many choices and actions can destroy a good reputation. Sometimes vicious people deliberately set out on a character assassination mission. The slanderer differs from a murderer only in that he kills the reputation rather than the body. A careless and foolish act can seriously damage one's reputation. White lies often leave black marks on a reputation. It takes a very short time to lose a good reputation but a extremely long time to regain it.

The bottom line is that "A good name is better than precious ointment as Ecclesiastes 7:1 explains. If you have a good reputation, you must be careful to protect and defend it. Let us not be guilty of saying or doing anything that would damage the good name of someone else.

Therefore, when I finally asked my students at the end of the unit what being a good human being means, they replied that it means thinking about others before you think about yourself, helping others without wanting something back for it, keeping a good name, and sharing what you have to help someone in need. I said that is very good, then posed a clarifying question, "Does being a good human being mean that you do the wrong things that you see others doing, like fighting or stealing?" After another highly engaged discussion, the class summarized that: 1) we need to do good things because this is the right thing to do. Just because a large number of people do something bad, it does not make it right; 2) being a good human being means that you do your best in your studies, in what you choose to do as a career, in your family, and in your community; 3) you must work hard to excel in your chosen field; and 4) never compromise on having good character.

Back in the day, it was often said: "His word is as good as his signature." That said, the phrase "good name" in Proverbs 22:1 implies far more than people would like it to represent. A good name infers someone who is honest, has good character, is a person of high integrity, someone who is a good credit risk, who has a good credit name, a good business reputation and is worthy of being hired for a new job. Truly, a good name is more preferred than money, in my humble opinion. After all, money cannot give a person a good name, no matter how much money one has, but a good name can garner money for a deserving person. Surely, if someone does not have both a good name and money, it may arguably be more preferable to have a good name and the peace that accompanies it, rather than money and the misery that usually is in fast company with it. Therefore, I have taught children early in their lives to seek a good name above all.

Additionally, I would suggest that teaching financial wisdom, specifically gaining and having a good credit name, become a necessary part of all school curricula so that students can learn to choose being debt free rather than accruing more indebtedness than they can possibly pay off during their lives. Children should be taught by their parents how to balance a checkbook, manage a budget, control their spending, differentiate needs and wants, and learn that a debt gained must become a debt paid off, and that debts should be paid on or well before the due date. In this way, care can be properly exercised about taking on obligations that cannot be easily met. The value of good credit must also be taught, for this is a true asset that is priceless. Newly married couples have a better chance at having a successful marriage, according to financial experts, when they establish good credit immediately upon marriage. I have heard it advised for individuals as well as young couples to borrow one hundred dollars from a bank, then pay it back within a week, and continue borrowing fifty dollars more each time, and paying that amount back within a few days until the borrowing limit has been reached. Another suggestion is usually made to buy a small number of items on credit from companies to establish good credit. This process strengthens both one's credit standing as well as one's credit rating, which will certainly come in handy as life's challenges are likely to occur.

Equally important in a person's development is realizing that one's family name should be held in the highest reputation by taking pride in having a good name, as well as in having a good family name. Just as there is school spirit, there should also be a family spirit. As an educator, I saw many students learn that when they did something good, that action brought pride to their parents and relatives. By the same token, those students who chose to do something wrong, realized that their choice of actions reflected negatively on their family. One's name and reputation should be highly valued by a life that is lived in the highest esteem.

This is done by teaching that earning a good name also includes avoiding evil at all cost, even avoiding the mere appearance of evil. One's character and reputation are vital: it's been said that character is what you are and your reputation is what others think you are. Even with the advent of social media, it is clearly noticed that how one is viewed can affect them and their family significantly. We must remember that one's name can be improved by fulfilling promises made, being dependable and punctual, completing responsibilities in a timely manner and serving others. For example, promises must not be taken lightly or with an air of indifference; instead, children should be taught that promises are to be made and upheld seriously and soberly. Conversely, someone's name can be ruined not only by doing something wrong, but also by failing to avoid the ever prevalent evil that surrounds us daily.

Speaking of a good name leads me to consider having a good heritage. There are many who give their children money but do not instruct them in having and maintaining a good character in order to prevent them from squandering the money, or spending like water. I believe that the best things to inherit from our elders are a good name, wisdom, faith in God, integrity and a great work ethic. Once inherited, these should be guarded with the utmost care so that the children can pass these priceless traits down to future generations.

May my students and my readers remember these values and make them their foundation for living, despite the negative impact from peers and the world observed around us. Children are living in an environment in which many people want to get rich quickly, have fame at any cost and have lots of material things. Negatively, peers are pressuring the young and even those who are older to develop habits and lifestyles that are destructive and even fatal. Peer pressure plays a dominant role in forming values throughout our lives, yet it is particularly central in the formative years. Let us lead by example and lay a firm foundation of faith and core values in our children. The future of the world and life as we know it depends on this.

BE GIFTED

Realize that we each have certain gifts, as well as developed talents. Use and share your gifts. Do not worry about what the critics say when you use your gifts:

"It is not the critic who counts, nor the man who points out how the strong man stumbles, or where the doer of deeds could have done better. Surely, the credit belongs to the man or woman who is actually in the arena, giving their all in the moment, whose face is marred by dust and sweat and blood, who strives valiantly, who errs and comes up short again and again, because there is no effort without error or shortcoming, but who knows the great enthusiasms, the great devotions, who spends himself for a worthy cause; who, at the best, knows in the end the triumph of high achievement, and who, at the worst, if he fails, at least he fails while daring greatly, so that his place shall never be with those cold and timid souls who knew neither victory nor defeat."

This is a paraphrase of Theodore Roosevelt's speech at the Sorbonne in 1910, yet he could have just as easily been speaking to you or me.

Those critics, those naysayers, the nags and the negative people in our lives who want to tell us: "No. It can't be done. Don't try. Give up. You are only doing this because someone else is in control of you. You don't have the guts to do this yourself. Why do you have to stand out? Why won't you just be sensible and give in to the inevitable?" These naysayers, critics and those who are constantly negative do not count. Refuse to mistake their words for the truth. Do not buy into their message to quit, settle for mediocrity and certainly do not give in to any form of underachievement.

Because we all have been blessed with talent, and we've had the fortune to live in this place at this time, we should choose to be one of the purposeful change agents in this land, for we have a higher calling. Who knows but God: perhaps we were placed here to be a benefit for such a time as this?

Personally, the people who matter to me are the ones who love me unconditionally, stand by me no matter what, and understand my great enthusiasms, devotions, struggles, prayers, purposes and pursuits. These are the ones who know that I spend myself daily for a worthy cause; who know that in the end, for me, it is all about the triumph of high achievement, helping others along the way and they cheer me on, knowing that I dared greatly to make a difference in this world. If even one person's life is made better because of my humble efforts, then my life shall not be in vain. The same may be true of you also.

Therefore let us each use the great gifts we have been given, find the forum where our talents will shine, make a difference while we can, and discover that place where our spirit soars. Let us get busy where the work smells like joy in the morning, as we enjoy each moment. Let us write the pages of our lives with each thought, choice, habit and action that we take, for we each are a blank page, writing on our life page with each choice. Prayerfully let God illuminate you as He shines within you, creating you into the Masterpiece of His divine purpose.

Be Wise:
Wise Counsel, Wise Choices

Each day of our lives we each are faced with various choices. What should we do before making an important choice and who should we take advice from? When life presents me with such questions, I consider the Bible as my primary source of wise counsel, as well as seeking advice from my inner circle of trusted friends, to assure that my choices honor God as well as others. However, there are times when the Bible does not seem to speak directly to the particular situations that are faced and the decisions that must me made. For that reason, the following ten principles enable each of us to make wise choices or decisions that glorify God and honor others.

1. What Biblical Principles Should Guide My Choice?

Consider these questions:

    a. What does the Bible have to say about that?

    b. Who can help me better understand what God's Word says about this decision?

    c. Make sure you are not the only one who holds to your interpretation.

Biblical Principles of Wisdom and Guidance

1 Corinthians 10:31

"So, whether you eat or drink, or whatever you do, do all to the glory of God."

Proverbs 2:6

"For the Lord gives wisdom; from His mouth comes knowledge and understanding."

Proverbs 12:15

The way of a fool is right in his own eyes, but a wise man listens to advice.

Proverbs 1:5

Let the wise hear and increase in learning, and the one who understands obtain guidance.

Proverbs 15:22

Without counsel plans fail, but with many advisers they succeed.

Proverbs 16:9

The heart of man plans his way, but the Lord establishes his steps.

Proverbs 3:5-6

"Trust in the Lord with all of your heart and do not lean on your own understanding. In all your ways acknowledge Him, and He will make your paths straight."

1 Peter 5:8

Be sober-minded; be watchful. Your adversary the devil prowls around like a roaring lion, seeking someone to devour.

Hebrews 11:1

Now faith is the assurance of things hoped for, the conviction of things not seen.

Psalm 119:9

How can a young man keep his way pure? By guarding it according to your word.

Joshua 1:9

Have I not commanded you? Be strong and courageous. Do not be frightened, and do not be dismayed, for the Lord your God is with you wherever you go."

1 Peter 5:8

Be sober-minded; be watchful. Your adversary the devil prowls around like a roaring lion, seeking someone to devour.

Matthew 6:24

"No one can serve two masters, for either he will hate the one and love the other, or he will be devoted to the one and despise the other. You cannot serve God and money.

Proverbs 13:11

Wealth gained hastily will dwindle, but whoever gathers little by little will increase it.

Hebrews 13:5

Keep your life free from the love of money, and be content with what you have, for he has said, "I will never leave you nor forsake you."

1 Timothy 5:8

But if anyone does not provide for his relatives, and especially for members of his household, he has denied the faith and is worse than an unbeliever.

1 Timothy 6:10

For the love of money is a root of all kinds of evils. It is through this craving that some have wandered away from the faith and pierced themselves with many pangs.

Proverbs 22:7

"The rich rules over the poor, and the borrower becomes the lender's slave."

2 Corinthians 6:14

"Do not be unequally yoked with unbelievers. For what partnership has righteousness with lawlessness? Or what fellowship has light with darkness?"

Philippians 4:8

"Finally, brethren, whatever is true, whatever is honorable, whatever is right, whatever is pure, whatever is lovely, whatever is of good repute, if there is any excellence and if anything worthy of praise, dwell on these things."

2. Do I Have All The Facts to Make My Choice?

Proverbs 18:13

"He who gives an answer before he hears, it is folly and shame to him."

Proverbs 18:17

"The first to plead his case seems right, until another comes and examines him."

Questions To Consider

1. Ask a lot of questions.

2. Don't fall prey to "wishful thinking" or let your emotions get the best of you.

3. Remember that there are two sides to every story.

3. Is The Pressure Of Time Forcing Me To Make A Premature Choice?

Proverbs 19:2

"Also it is not good for a person to be without knowledge, and he who makes haste with his feet errs."

Proverbs 21:5

"The plans of the diligent lead surely to advantage, but everyone who is hasty comes surely to poverty."

Questions To Consider

1. Beware of the "once in a life time" deal and the lure of instant gratification.

2. Don't let the fear of missing out drive your decision.

3. When in doubt, leave it out.

4. What Possible Motives Are Driving My Choice?

Proverbs 16:2

"All the ways of a man are clean in his own sight, but the Lord weighs the motives."

Proverbs 20:9

"Who can say, 'I have cleansed my heart, I am pure from my sin?'"

Questions To Consider

1. Acknowledge that you have "blind spots."

2. Honestly assess your motives, both good and bad.

3. Give others permission to speak in to your life.

5. How Should Past Experiences Inform My Decision?

Proverbs 26:11

"Like a dog that returns to its vomit is a fool who repeats his folly."

Proverbs 17:10

"A rebuke goes deeper into one who has understanding than a hundred blows into a fool."

Questions To Consider

1. Look for patterns of behavior or "trigger points."

2. Understand how your family background might affect your thinking.

3. Learn from your mistakes!

6. What Is The Wise Counsel of My Community?

Proverbs 11:14

"Where there is no guidance the people fall, but in an abundance of counselors there is victory."

Proverbs 18:1

"He who separates himself seeks his own desire. He quarrels against all sound wisdom."

Proverbs 18:2

"A fool does not delight in understanding, but only in revealing his own mind."

Questions To Consider

1. Avoid having many separate conversations.

2. Recognize the difference between "selling" and "sharing."

3. Know when to open and close the circle of counsel.

7. Have I Honestly Considered All of the Warning Signs of My Choice?

Proverbs 10:17

"He is on the path of life who heeds instruction, but he who forsakes reproof goes astray."

Proverbs 16:25

"There is a way which seems right to a man, but its end is the way of death."

Proverbs 27:6

"Faithful are the wounds of a friend, but deceitful are the kisses of an enemy."

Questions To Consider

1. Don't think you are the "exception" to the rule.

2. Remember that God's way is the best way.

8. Have I Honestly Considered Every Possible Outcome For My Chosen Course Of Action?

Proverbs 14:1

"The wise woman builds her house, but the foolish tears it down with her own hands."

Proverbs 14:15

"The naïve believes everything, but the prudent man considers his steps."

Proverbs 27:12

"A prudent man sees evil and hides himself, the naïve proceed and pay the penalty."

Questions To Consider

1. Do the "long math," realize what lies ahead on the path of your choice.

2. Assess the potential risks.

3. Have a contingency or back up plan.

9. Could This Choice Jeopardize My Integrity or Hinder My Witness For The Lord?

Proverbs 10:9

"He who walks in integrity walks securely, but he who perverts his ways will be found out."

Proverbs 20:7

"A righteous man who walks in his integrity—how blessed are his sons after him."

Proverbs 25:26

"Like a trampled spring and a polluted well is a righteous man who gives way before the wicked."

Proverbs 22:1

"A good name is to be more desired than great riches, favor is better than silver and gold."

Questions To Consider

1. Work toward the center of purpose rather than flirt with the risky edge.

2. Ask yourself, would this pass the "newspaper" test? If it were reported on the front page of the local newspaper, would your chosen course of action be considered as either improper behavior or embarrassing behavior?

3. Keep short accounts.

10. Is There A Better Choice That Would Allow Me To Make A Greater Impact For God's Kingdom?

Proverbs 11:30

"The fruit of the righteous is a tree of life, and he who is wise wins souls."

Questions To Ask

1. Ask yourself, what story could God be writing?

2. Don't assume that just because something is hard that it is not God's will.

3. Understand how God has uniquely gifted and resourced you.

Be Strengthened: Laugh!

Our mouths were filled with laughter, our tongues with songs of joy. Then it was said among the nations, "The Lord has done great things for them." The Lord has done great things for us, and we are filled with joy. –Psalm 126:2-3

Sometimes, no matter how bad things look, remember that this is only temporary, for you will get through this. Let nothing steal your joy. Instead, be grateful by counting your blessings. This will give you a fresh outlook as you realize all the great things God has done, is doing and will do on your behalf. Sometimes, you just have to take the time to laugh and rejoice. That's right, I said, "Laugh and rejoice." Let me tell you the reasons why. In Nehemiah 8:10 it says, " This day is holy to our Lord. Do not grieve, for **the joy of the Lord is your strength**." Did you also know that in Proverbs 17:22, Solomon wrote, "**a cheerful heart is good medicine,** but a crushed spirit dries up the bones?" Here in the pages of God's holy Word are clearly explained benefits of having a merry heart. Certainly, there are times in our lives that are full of disappointment, sickness, sadness, sorrow and discouragement, yet our heavenly Father God did not design us to live lives of gloom and doom for us to be sick and tired of being sick and tired too soon. In no way am I minimizing the dark times of our lives. Instead, as a faith-filled Christian, I am pointing out that through the abiding strength of the Lord we have the ability to rise above such discouragements.

I know of people who have battled serious illnesses and tough situations. You would expect someone suffering such difficulties to be pessimistic, discouraged and an outlook more sour than a lemon, like a coworker I used to work with. Some people you don't dare ask how they are doing unless you are prepared to hear a long laundry list of what is wrong in their lives, and their answer could take all day!

Then there are others who you may have noticed who are a joy to be around, always with a positive outlook and an optimistic persona, just happy all the time. Sure, I've had my share of ups and downs just like everybody else, but I hold on to God's promises with the assurance that, just like many times before, He will bring me through all right. He has never left me, in fact, I can rely on Him always being right there with me, helping me through all that has happened.

Truth is, as the adage goes, "you are not what you think you are, but you are what you think." Basically, people are either cheerful or not because they choose that lifestyle. As Solomon observed in Proverbs 23:7, "As he thinks in his heart, so is he," and in Proverbs 4:23, "Keep your heart with all diligence; for out of it are the issues of life." Herein are two points of emphasis noting the fundamental necessity of proper thinking and its impact on every aspect of our lives.

There is no mystery in the realization that how a person thinks directly impacts the body's organs. Just tell someone that it is their duty to make a presentation and a speech in a large public setting and watch how they react: most likely, with a flushed face, an apparent nervousness, sweaty palms and brow, and an increased heart rate as adrenalin flows more rapidly. This person may even become ill because of intense fear of this task. Why? Because their thinking has affected their health. Over the years, medical research has extensively proven that stress and anxiety have a direct effect on the human body's wellness. Did you know that this includes disorders of the glands, the nervous system, the inflammatory system, the circulatory system, the genito-urinary system, infections, allergic disorders, muscle-joint disorders, drug and nutritional disorders and even cancer? How one thinks is not the only cause, given that genetics and one's contact with bacteria, disease, accidents and other possible factors, obviously play a significant part. Of course, life will have its times of sadness and stress, for just as we notice in the weather, sometimes there is sunshine, other times there's rain and thunderstorms. Even Jesus wept in John 11:30, got angry and was even grieved, as noted in Mark 3:5. Also, God our heavenly Father, His son Jesus Christ and the

Holy Spirit can be grieved, according to Ephesians 4:30, Mark 3:5 and Genesis 6:6. So, do not feel guilty when these feelings arise. They are normal for the triune God and they are normal for us too. Still, why not control what you can control by changing your perspective on life? Choose, as Solomon suggested from his observances and experiences, to be inspired rather than depressed by life's seasons, as noted in Ecclesiastes 3:1-8:

To everything there is a season, and a time to everyty purpose under the heaven: A time to be born, and a time to die; a time to plant, and atime to pluck up that which is planted; A time to weep, and a time to laugh; A time to mourn, and a time to dance; A tiome to cast away stones, and a time to gather stone together; A time to embrace, and a time to refrain from embracing; A time to get, and a time to lose; A time to keep, and a time to cast away; A time to rend (rip), and a time to sew; A time to keep silence, and a time to speak; A time to love, and a time to hate; A time of war, and time of peace.

Here we see that **all emotions** have their proper place, yet the negative emotions must not and should not dominate our lives. In John 10:10, Jesus said, *"The thief comes to steal and to kill and to destroy; I am come that they might have life, and that they might have it more abundantly."* Despite living in a world filled with doom and gloom, let us choose to be of good cheer, for the Lord Jesus taught us in John 16:33, *"These things I have spoken to you that in Me yoiu might have peace. In the world, you will have tribulation; But be of good cheer; I have overcome the world."*

Consequently, having a cheery disposition and a sunny outlook changes your attitude, your health and your life, in addition to impacting everyone you encounter. For example, at work, when I would cheerfully say to a certain coworker who will remain nameless, "Good morning, how are you today?" she would bark back at me with a sneering growl, "Arrrgggghhh! What's good about it?" and march off to her class like she was ready to chew rocks and spit them out. Yet there were others, like my students, their parents and other coworkers, who saw my sunny outlook as an encouragement to what they were going through. Therefore, what I'm sharing is that each one can reach one, so let us lift each other up. Just a smile can change someone's day. Why not start today by smiling at yourself in the mirror, then smile at others? Now here is something to get you started. I heard these funny stories on the radio. Hope each one tickles your funny bone!

A doctor, a lawyer, a little boy and a priest were out for a Sunday afternoon flight on a small private plane. Suddenly, the plane developed engine trouble. In spite of the best efforts of the pilot, the plane started to go down. Finally, the pilot grabbed a parachute, yelled to the passengers that they had better jump, and then he bailed out.

Unfortunately, there were only three parachutes remaining. So, the doctor grabbed one and said "I'm a doctor, I save lives, so I must live," then he jumped out.

The lawyer then said, "I'm a lawyer. Since lawyers are the smartest people in the world, I deserve to live." He also grabbed a parachute and jumped.

The priest looked at the little boy and said, "My son, I've lived a long and full life. You are young and have your whole life ahead of you. Take the last parachute, be well and may you always live in peace."

The little boy handed the parachute back to the priest and said, "Do not worry, Father. The smartest man in the world just took off with my back pack!

***

As a retired educator, I find these chemical descriptions particularly hilarious. Enjoy!

Element: WOMAN Symbol: Wo

Atomic Weight: 135 (more or less, usually more)

Physical Properties: Generally round in form. Boils at nothing and may freeze anytime. Melts whenever treated properly. Very bitter if not used well.

Chemical Properties: Very active. Highly unstable. Possesses strong affinity to gold, silver, platinum and precious stones. May become violent when left alone for extended periods of time. Able to absorb great amounts of exotic food. Turns slightly green when placed next to a better specimen. Ages rapidly without healthy habits.

Usage: Highly productive and compassionate. Some are purely ornamental. Some varieties are able to support immense pressure yet remain positive, while others are likely to be more fragile. Certain varieties are combustible and can also get extremely bent when heated or treated improperly. Do not take for granted. Responds best to consistent, tender loving care.

Caution: Highly explosive in inexperienced hands. Operate at your own risk. Certain varieties are an extremely good catalyst for dispersion of wealth. Probably the most powerful income reducing agent known.

Element: MAN Symbol: XY

Atomic Weight: 180 (+/- 100)

Physical Properties: Solid at room temperature, but gets bent out of shape when heated. Fairly dense and sometimes flaky. Difficult to find a pure sample. Due to rust, aging samples are unable to conduct electricity as easily as young fresh samples.

Chemical Properties: Attempts to bond with Wo any chance it can get. Also, tends to form strong bonds with itself. Becomes explosive when mixed with stupidity (element Stupidity), alcohol or Kd (element Kid) for prolonged periods of time. Pretty basic. Neutralize by saturating with consistent, tender loving care.

Usage: Some varieties are able to support immense pressure yet remain positive. At its best when combined with Wo. Really excels at profuse methane production. Good samples are able to produce large quantities on demand.

Caution: In the absence of Wo, this element rapidly decomposes and begins to smell. Ages rapidly without consistent healthy habits.

***

A certain senior confessed: I have recently been diagnosed with AAADD - Age Activated Attention Deficit Disorder. What exactly is Age Activated Attention Deficit Disorder? This is how it is on a daily basis:

I decide to wash the car. I start toward the garage and notice the mail on the table. OK, I'm going to wash the car, but first, I'm going to go through the mail.

I lay the car keys down on the desk, discard the junk mail, and notice the trash can is full. OK, I'll just put the bills on the desk and take the trash out, but since I'm going to be near the mailbox anyway, I'll pay these few bills first.

Now where is the checkbook? Oops, there's only one check left. My extra checks are in the desk. As I start looking for the checks, I see the coke I was drinking sitting on the desk...I'm going to look for those checks...

Oh, but first I need to put my coke further away from the computer. Oh, maybe I'll pop it into the fridge to keep it cold for a while. I head toward the kitchen and the plants catch my eye, they need some water. I set the coke on the counter and uh oh! There are my glasses. I was looking for them all morning! I'm pretty sure I really don't have age activated attention deficit disorder!

Now I'd better put the glasses away first. I fill a container with water and head for the flowerpots-Aaaaaargh! Someone left the TV remote in the kitchen. We'll never think to look in the kitchen tonight when we want to watch television, so I'd better put it back in the family room where it belongs.

So, I splash some water into the pots and onto the floor, I throw the remote onto a soft cushion on the sofa and I head back down the hall trying to figure out what it was I was going to do...!!??!! Surely this is not any type of an aging disorder, or deficit, or anything like that, I think.

Finally, it's the end of the day. The car still isn't washed, the bills are still unpaid, the coke is still sitting on the kitchen counter, the flowers are only half watered, the checkbook still only has one check in it and I still can't seem to find my car keys anywhere!

When I try to figure out why in the world nothing got done today, I'm baffled because I know good and well that I was busy all day long!!! Now I definitely realize this Age Activated Attention Deficit Disorder is a serious condition, so I'd better get some help, but first, I think I'll check my e-mail.

***

Oh, the unique challenges awaiting the woman who is approaching middle age! Imagine, despite all your hard labor workouts, healthier eating plans and lifestyle management, waking up one morning to find your face sort of lying in a pool beside you. Your once tight abs have been replaced with something rather squishy that has to be gathered up, starting somewhere around the knees, and tucked into industrial-strength, control-top Spanx, whole body girdles and pantyhose, all ready to plop out with a huge sigh of relief once you finally wiggle and pop out of all that constricted madness, totally exhausted from squeezing into it then managing to squeeze out of it. Imagine suddenly realizing that your cellulite thighs almost create sparks when you walk. Your biceps are so deflated that in a strong breeze you worry that they might actually make a flapping sound like a flag. Maybe you do not have to imagine any of this. Maybe you are a living example of it.

God might have knit these earthly bodies together out of a more "permanent press" kind of fabric. He could have built in a kind of

116

stretch that wouldn't lose its elasticity around middle age but he didn't. Through our aging and all the challenges we live through, He faithfully teaches us what is really important.

The Proverbs 31 "wife of noble character" got in on that teaching. She could "laugh at the days to come" (verse 25). Her future held flabby abs, arms and combustible thighs too. Yet still, she could laugh. Why?

Herein the passage describes a woman who seems just about perfect. Many Bible teachers call her the "virtuous woman," and she makes Martha Stewart look like a novice. She keeps her husband happy; she works eagerly; she gets up early and stays up late. Her husband's heart trusts in her. She gives to others generously. She is so creative that she makes her own clothes. She is an eloquent teacher and her kids love her. A woman like this "who can find," indeed! She is a formidable pattern of life and certainly an example of excellence, inspiring many women's aspirations, someone to become with God's help as He shapes our lives through varied experiences, for He is the Potter, we are the clay.

Consider it pure joy, my brothers, whenever you face trials of many kinds, because you know that the testing of your faith devleops perseverance. Perseverance must finish its work so thatyou may be mature and complete, not lacking anything. –James 1:2-4

However, let us look past the outward layer. Look deeper. Here you will see a woman of wisdom who fully understood what was really important in life. She was not consumed with the foolishness of the day nor the culture she lived in. She chose to be peculiarly different, a woman of purpose. She understood what it meant to work hard, give her best, love sincerely and serve God with her whole heart. She understood that everything of consequence was wrapped up in The Lord. Therefore, serving others came as a natural extension of serving Him.

These days, many are seeking a total makeover. There are style consultants who outfit you and your environment to look more posh, sophisticated, professional and well put together. There are others who makeover a person from head to toe, and transform how he or she thinks and speaks in order to build up their confidence in their daily interactions. Truly, to God, only one metamorphosis really matters, and it will keep every woman eternally beautiful. It is the transformation of the heart. Scripture says in 2 Corinthians 5:17, *"Therefore, if anyone is in Christ, the new creation has come: The old has gone, the new is here!"* Having a heart of unselfish, loving service that has been transformed by Christ is far more important. That is what gives us the ability to laugh at the future, even if it involves having flabby arms and thighs.

Reflection

When your attention to appearance gets out of whack and your focus is more on looks than on eternal things, how might "fearing the Lord" turn your focus back to where it needs to be?

What are some of the ways the woman in Proverbs 31:10-31 served others?

How many different types of people did her daily life and ministry touch? How might you underestimate the many lives you touch each day?

She is clothed with strength and dignity; she can laugh at the days to come. Charm is deceptive, and beauty is fleeting; but a woman who fears the LORD is to be praised. - Proverbs 31:25, 30

Psalm 139:1-24; Romans 12:1-13; Galatians 6:9-10; 1 Peter 3:1-6

Be Youthful and Refreshed

Surely, we all have those trying, disturbing, up and down life experiences that make us feel upside down, turned inside out, and topsy turvy, just like being on an out of control rollercoaster. More often than not, those difficult circumstances weigh us down physically, emotionally, mentally and spiritually. However, it is up to each of us to choose to be uplifted and strengthened. This decision enables us to overcome those tough times and that infuses us with a youthful yet wise effervescence that is decidedly maintained through an optimistic outlook as we strategically work through trials. We do what is required to reach resolution yet maintain our joy and strength.

What Do I Do to Stay Young?

People often ask me the reasons for my youthful appearance. Here are a few gems that hopefully will be your "fountain of youth."

1. Make leisure time, play time and enjoyment a top priority. I take time to laugh at myself, at comedians, or at some favorite situation comedies. I definitely laugh often at funny movies. Remember "I Love Lucy," "Ma and Pa Kettle," "The Johnsons' Vacation," "Mr. Bean," Sinbad, Bill Cosby and Steve Harvey? These are just a few of the many assets in my humor tool kit.

2. Make time to have fun. Crack a joke or listen to good jokes. Have a good belly laugh. Play a game. Watch your children and grandchildren when they are playing, better yet, play with them. Enjoy something pleasant and relaxing that makes you smile. Get together with a great friend or relative for some warm, refreshing hang out time. Share a mutually enjoyable activity with your significant other. Take a scenic drive and stop to have a picnic at a favorite spot. Take a trip, whether it's a day trip, a drive across the nation, or an international jaunt. Just get out and see what's around you, for you may be pleasantly surprised by what you find. Enjoy a musical, a play or a concert. Change your venue by getting out of that house, condo, hotel room or apartment. Go out to a favorite eatery, even if it's just to have some great sweet tea or the perfect glass of lemonade. Put some upbeat music on and dance. All of these are likely choices for me. Another is having a good cup of tea and pastry with either a good book or a wonderful movie while relaxing in my favorite easy chair does it for me. Whatever you choose to do, enjoy life, for as John 10:10 says, "I (Jesus) came so that you may have life and have it more abundantly." Also, I enjoy going to a park and getting on the swings. It is so rejuvenating to feel the breeze on my skin as I fly with my feet in the air, trying to touch the clouds. Truly, this is the image of being carefree.

3. Try everything delightful twice. On one woman's tombstone, she said that she wanted this epitaph: "Tried everything twice. Loved it both times!" Personally, good music, art and literature inspire and encourage me. Great music of all genres with meaningful lyrics speak to my heart and energize me. Inspirational music, anecdotal humor and stories of faith such as I've found on 95.9 FM, The Fish and 99.5FM, KKLA really get add fuel to my joy tank.

4. Keep only positive, cheerful, productive friends. The ones who repeatedly pour out their problems to you without 1) listening to any of your sound advice and 2) without ever listening supportively to you can wear you out and make you feel so weighed down that you have difficulty picking yourself back up. Additionally heavy to carry are hte naysayers and those who are constantly negative every time you speak with them, aka sour lemon grouches who can cause you to feel depressed and pull you down. You need people who are uplifting. Keep this in mind if you are one of those sourpuss grouches.

5. Never stop learning something new. Learn more about the new technology that is all around us. Go to a recently updated library and use their newer computers so that you can familiarize yourself with the new software. Just for 15 minutes, try a friend's smart phone, with their permission of course, to learn a new application that they downloaded so that you can have an idea if this is a smartphone you would like to buy. There are also so many new tablets, technologically advanced watches and other electronic devices, like the Kindle, to explore. Try out a new hobby to enjoy, for example, painting, gardening, cooking, crafts, interior decorating, or wherever your particular interests take you. Whatever you do, grow. Do not allow your mind to become idle. Do some puzzles, learn a new language, learn to play an instrument or do mental exercises to stay sharp. Always remember that an idle mind is the devil's workshop, and the devil's name is Alzheimers!

6. Be grateful to God every day. Find three things every day to be grateful for. Hey, you woke up today. Realize that you are alive, breathing and functioning. You have health and strength in whatever degree that you have them. These are gifts of grace, given to you, that you can never earn. If you are a believer, you have your life has been saved and you have the gift of eternal life. Look at all the difficulties and trials that God has brought you safely through. Think about all the dangers, seen and unseen, that you have been saved from.

7. Rejoice! Whoever you are, whatever you have, whatever you are able to do, wherever you are, whatever you have accomplished, rejoice at the growth thus far in your life. Think about all the people you are thankful for and their influences on your life. Look around you. Think about all the obstacles in life that you have overcome and rejoice.

8. Notice the beauty and resources all around you. Reflect on the serenity and the refreshment they bring. Look around you at all the wonders that God created. The sky, the earth, the plants and trees, every living and breathing thing, wildlife, flora and fauna, scenic places everywhere, art, music, creativity, the list can go on and on.

9. Live by faith, not by fear. God lays before us the paths we may choose to follow.

In Philippians 1:20, the optimistic Apostle Paul said, *"I live in eager expectation...while I'm going through these trials."* Conversely, in Job 2:24, pessimistic Job said, *"Everything I fear and dread comes true."* So staying optimistic is the key.

Start the day with prayer and praise: *"This is the day the Lord has made! Let us rejoice and be glad in it!"* Psalm 118:24; *"In the morning, O Lord, You hear my voice, in the morning, I lay my request before You and wait in expectation."* Ps 5:3

Look for good in your situation, as Romans 8:28 instructs, *"For those who love God, who are called according to His plan, <u>everything that happens fits into a pattern for good.</u>"*

Give your problems to the Lord, for *"He can even raise the dead. And He did help...and we expect Him to do it again and again."* 2 Corinthians 1:11. Base your optimism on your faith in Christ, for according to your faith, it will be done to you. Expect the best!

Take time to pray, read and study His Word, the Bible. Commit certain scripture verses to memory, to meditate on and feed your spirit throughout each day. Give thanks to God. Praise His holy name. Worship Him. Rejoice that God is faithful and keeps every promise that He made to us. Read the Bible to learn what those promises are. Speak them in prayer and praise, giving thanks to Him for His love.

10. Look on the bright side. Count your blessings instead of counting your worries. Have a grateful heart. Consider yourself blessed for the life, the things and the opportunities you have. Did you know that every day that is given, rather gifted to you, is a real blessing? You are breathing, alive, able to smile, move about and make choices. You are able to hug, love and be with others who are dear to you. You have abilities and skills that enable you to be creative as well as productive. You have been delivered from situations and people who

either intentionally or unintentionally meant you harm. Any blessings you are enjoying today should never be taken for granted. Realize that God has faithfully granted you His unmerited love, grace and mercy, extended to you freely, day in and day out. Every day, God's new mercies and favor are freely given to you. Stop taking these mercies and blessings for granted, for what is given today may not be given tomorrow. Tomorrow is not promised, but today is the present, a gift to be thankful for. Far too many people complain about everything and everyone under the sun. I choose to break that trend and just be grateful. Yes, I've had my share of ups and downs but no matter what has happened to me, for the good, the bad, questionable and the ugly are all instruments in the Potter's capable, creative hands to make me, and all those affected by my life, better. So I count myself blessed despite all the storms that life has brought, for I am still here and I continue to rise, a victor, and an overcomer by faith and perseverance.

7. Laugh loudly, laugh often, and laugh a long time. Laugh so hard until you are holding your side. Be filled with laughter. Find books, movies and events to laugh about. Laugh at your honest mistakes. Stop taking yourself and your life so seriously. Lighten up! There are even free sites on the Internet with funny stories and jokes. Find friends who make you laugh, find ways to make them laugh, then spend as much time as possible with them.

8. LIVE! When the tears happen, and they eventually will, remember this: Weep, endure, grieve, and push yourself to keep on moving forward. Face it. There is only one person who is with you your entire life: look in the mirror. It is you. You are with yourself all day long, all

night long, all week long, all month and all year, year after year. Make it a priority to live, enjoying each moment, while you are alive.

9. Surround yourself with everything that inspires, uplifts, motivates, rejuvenates, calms and strengthens you.

10. Your home is your refuge. Make it an oasis of serenity, harmony, peace and rest. When you come home, it should be a retreat for your mind, body, spirit and soul. Create a relaxing atmosphere with natural, serence colors and decorative accents. Where possible, include objects that are inspired by nature. Keep your space simple, rather than cluttered to allow the mind to be unstressed by too many things to look at which set off a trend of mental overstimulation. Try simple accents like potted plants, a small water fountain, an acquarium or wind chimes. Create CDs (compact discs) with hours of calm, relaxing instrumental music to help you unwind, particularly after a long or challenging day. Set up a quiet place of loveliness and stillness in your patio, deck or back yard. Set up a garden to reflect upon your blessings. Consider the relaxing motion of a rocking chair, hammock, hanging swing or an easy chair with a built in rocker.

11. Turn off your electronic devices for a set time and enjoy an atmosphere of daily quiet. Our world is far too noisy and intrusive. This is the time that I pray and praise God for all He is to me. I have been through storms but He brought me out. My money has been funny but He brought me out. I have been in tough situations, but He brought me out. I have been put in situations I haven't been trained for, but He has anointed me to do greater things as He works in and through me. I have been up and down, through thick and thin, from can't to can, but God brought me out. God helps me as I continually stay close in communion with Him. He is the reason that I am what I am, that I do what I do and that I rejoice because He is the Great I Am. This is why the quiet stillness is so vital to me because that is when He speaks to me in His Word, through the lyrics of a song, through others and speaks peace to me in nature.

12. Cherish, maintain and preserve your good health. Do what you are supposed to do. If your health is good, preserve it. If it is unstable, improve it. If it is beyond what you can do to improve it, then get the required professional help.

13. Never take guilt trips. They are like rocking chairs, taking you on a trip but never arriving at a desired destination. Instead, take a trip to the local aviary, the petting zoo, the museum, the shopping mall, the next county, another state, to a foreign country, but NOT to where the guilt is. Pack it up, throw it away and throw the key away too.

14. Tell and show your loved ones that you love them every chance you get. Do the little things that show you care.

15. Right now, forgive those who made you hurt and cry.

Forgiveness brings you freedom. You may not get a second chance.

Remember! Lost time can never be found.

God's Boxes

I have in my hands two boxes which God gave me to hold. He said, "Put all your sorrows in the black and all your joys in the gold. I heeded

His words. In the two boxes, both my joys and sorrows I stored but though the gold box became heavier each day, the black box was as light as before. With curiousity, I opened the black box, I so wanted to find out why, and I saw, in the base of the box, a hole which my sorrows had fallen out by!

I showed the hole to God and mused aloud, "I wonder where my sorrows could be." He smiled a gentle smile at me, saying, "My child, they are all with me." I asked Him, "God, why give me the boxes: why the gold, and the black with the hole?" He replied, "My child, the gold is for you to count your blessings. The black is for you to let go."

Let go, and let God!

Be kinder than necessary, for everyone you meet is going through some kind of trial, disappointment, or struggle. Realize the blessing of friendship and treasure the joy each one is in your life.

Wine does not make you F A T .... It makes you LEAN ....

against tables, chairs, floors, walls and ugly people.

Think before you drink.

BE A CONTINUAL LEARNER

Every footstep leave lasting impressions in the soil. Every thought is a seed. Before we allow a thought to be planted in our hearts, we must judge the spirit that brought that thought into our minds.

Wrong thoughts produce the seeds of wrong choices. Wrong choices produce the fruit of wrong actions. Wrong actions sprout up as weeds in the garden of a life that is not well tended. Weeds hold on so very tightly, with very deep root systems, that they are difficult to pull up. Let us be careful to read with discernment the people around us, and judge them by their fruits in order to correctly determine who they are and whose they are. Wisdom precedes action as we are governed by the guidance of the Holy Spirit.

Take the time to learn something new, for this keeps the mind growing stronger and, according to research, prevents Alzheimers. Learn a new language, a new form of technology, take a different route to work, learn new vocabulary or even, learn a new hobby. You'll be glad you did.

Here are some lessons that either I have already learned along the course of life, or that I am still doing the homework for as I put them into practice more regularly.

BE PURPOSEFUL: OTHER GARDENING TIPS

Gardening Tip #1: If you don't like where you're going, change the course.

That leads me to the next gardening tip: Instead of letting things and people get on your last nerve, then doing something antagonistic in return, don't. Instead, just stop it. Don't become another victim of road rage and the crazy unpredictable behavior that is standard conduct these days. Let the irritation slide off your back like water. Choose to just let it go, and by doing so, stay alive. Think about all your precious loved ones and go home to them, safely.

Gardening Tip #2: Decide to make someone else's day better; exercise good character.

Yes, there are still good people around, and you can choose to be one of them.

Gardening Tip #3: Get quiet, be still, and let creativity flow.

Have you ever noticed how difficult it is to think when constant noise is around you? Sometimes you are in a place where you are unable to control the noise, but you can control your intake of it. Do as I do: either get up and take a walk, go to a quiet place for a few moments or put your ear buds on, get up earlier to enjoy the peaceful quiet, turn on some peaceful music and watch how productive you become by removing the annoyance.

Gardening Tip #4: Remain hopeful and inspired by God's Word.

Proverbs 24:14 *Know that wisdom is such to your soul; if you find it, there will be a future, and your hope will not be cut off.*

Jeremiah 29:11 *For I know the plans I have for you, declares the LORD, plans for welfare and not for evil, to give you a future and a hope.*

Titus 1:1-2 *Paul, a servant of God and an apostle of Jesus Christ, for the sake of the faith of God's elect and their knowledge of the truth, which accords with Godliness, in hope of eternal life, which God, who never lies, promised before the ages began.*

Titus 3:7 *so that being justified by his grace we might become heirs according to the hope of eternal life.*

1 Corinthians 15:19 *If in Christ we have hope in this life only, we are of all people most to be pitied.*

2 Corinthians 4:16-18 *So we do not lose heart. Though our outer self is wasting away, our inner self is being renewed day by day. For this light momentary affliction is preparing for us an eternal weight of glory beyond all comparison, as we look not to the things that are seen but to the things that are unseen. For the things that are seen are transient, but the things that are unseen are eternal.*

1 Peter 1:3 *Blessed be the God and Father of our Lord Jesus Christ! According to his great mercy, he has caused us to be born again to a living hope through the resurrection of Jesus Christ from the dead,*

Gardening Tip #5: Get out and get moving. Exercise and fresh air are great toners for life.

Gardening Tip #6: Research and study to learn something new.

Gardening Tip #7: Are you thriving or surviving with OPC?

Gardening Tip #8: Take the time to add wisdom and beauty to life. Therefore, I share this poem I penned:

Gardening for Life Blues

Written by Vicki Evans

© Marvic Music

Life is like a garden. All you sow, you will reap. Life is like a garden. All you sow, you will reap.

Every intention has a purpose and every purpose plays for keeps.

Weed your garden, baby. Let wisdom's light shine on through. Weed your garden, baby. Let love and wisdom shine in you. Keep your life in the Light, So those evil weeds don't consume you.

BE OPTIMISTICALLY FOCUSSED: SEEING THE GLASS AS FULL BY CHOICE

There is an age old argument that, hypothetically, one either sees the glass as half empty or half full. Actually, I opine that the glass is full either way: half full of whatever substance it contains and half full of oxygen. Though it may be invisible, nonetheless the air is there. That is a realization that is often overlooked in that discussion. This is what I mean by being optimistically focused, intentionally looking for the good and doing good.

Optimists look for the light at the end of the tunnel. If you've always had a pessimistic worldview, it can be difficult to shift your focus, but it is possible to at least start seeing the glass as half full, not half empty. In fact, the reality is that glasses are generally all full: it's just that gravity tends to attract the more dense liquid material towards the bottom.

While for some, being skeptical can be viewed as a healthy way to avoid getting taken advantage of, being pessimistic or always assuming the worst, can definitely have major negative consequences on your life. Not only can seeing only the negative aspects of a situation cause you to miss wonderful opportunities, being pessimistic can also cause you to neglect problems that need to be solved, and fail to take actions that would otherwise improve your relationships and quality of life. In fact, studies show that pessimists are more likely to develop chronic illnesses more often later in life than optimists.

Instead, choose optimism as a way of life.

Action Steps to Optimism

1. Let go of the assumption that the world is against you, or that you were born with a gray cloud over your head. It is an assumption that has no basis in reason or science. Sometimes we pick up a flair for pessimism from a parent, friend or acquaintance who regularly made negative assumptions about people and the world somewhere along the line. Either way, the sooner you can attribute your pessimism to a unique set of circumstances rather than the state of the world itself, the easier it will be to change your perspective.

2. Understand that the past does not equal the future. Just because you've experienced pain or disappointment in the past does not guarantee that what starts badly will end badly. Do not make a bad start turn into a self fulfilling prophecy for a bad ending.

3. See yourself as a cause, not an effect. You don't have to be a product or a victim of your circumstances. Stop thinking about what happened to you and start thinking about what you can make happen. If you're not happy with the way your life is now, set goals and move on. Use your past negative experiences to build character and make better decisions. Life involves taking many risks every day, and not all of them will end positively. That's what defines risk. But the flip side is that some actions will lead to good results, and it's generally better to have a mixed bag than to have nothing at all. Ideally, the good stuff will outweigh the bad, but you'll never reach that point unless you put yourself out there and hope.

4. Daily use positive affirmations. Write down scriptures, witty sayings and short statements that remind you of what you're trying to change about the way you see the world. Put them in places where you'll see them every day, such as on your bathroom mirror, the inside of your locker, on your computer monitor, and even taped to your shower wall.

BE GLAD FOR THE BEST DAY EVER

I just woke up
And I realized
It's the best day ever
Of my glorious life

First of all
I am alive
What a gift
Lord I give You a high five!

Didn't have to wake up
Coulda been dead
But God saw fit
To give me life instead

Got out of bed
Grateful and glad
That I'm moving my body
No pain, no feeling bad

Looked in the mirror
Look at me!

LIVE SUNNY SIDE UP!

I am so thankful
That I can see!

Opened my mouth
Said "Thank You Lord"
For the ability to even
Say a single word

Looked all around me
With a smile on my face
Just to have some food
And not be hungry in this place

Looked up above me
And began to cry
For this roof over my head
Not on the street to die

Looked in my pocket
How I rejoice
There's money in there
Help me make a wise choice

Tears are flowing
Oh my, I can hear

Clock ticking, birds singing
With my open, working ears

My heart is so happy
To love and be loved
As evidenced daily
By all these gifts from above

Peace and joy
Just happy to be
It's the best day ever
Full of opportunity!
Written by Vicki Evans
Copyright Marvic Music

Start each day with joy and unending gratitude.

No matter how easy it is to grumble, to shuffle groggily and to moan in complaint, instead choose to use that same energy to:

Smile, rejoice, laugh and be grateful!

As my song says, think of all that you can give thanks to God for. A brand new day of life. Air to breathe, the ability to make a difference, people who care about you, and so much more if you just think about it. Make it a habit to count your blessings instead of counting your sorrows. You are here. Life is a gift. What to you do with gifts? Whine and speak negatively? Of course not! Rejoice, show gratitude. You have a purpose, and a chance to make a difference in others' lives.

So, get after it. Fun, grateful, positive, productive and healthy thoughts are not merely for children, you know -- or only for the rich -- nor only for the happy go lucky. You need fun, joy, purpose, love and laughter as much as you need air and food!

Maybe you feel that each day seems alike, dull, gray and grim. Maybe you are irritated by the little things, as you drag yourself to do one task after another. Maybe you isolate yourself from people as I used to do back in the day, for a variety of reasons, maybe thinking about the wrongs that have been done to you, choosing not to "be so bothered with people." Maybe as you look in your mailbox, you then wonder why the invitations stop coming. Maybe you really aren't really sick but you're far from feeling well. Well, whatever the maybes are in your life, choose to stop and retool your thinking. For all you know, things are not as grim as they seem. Just the other day, I was driving to work. Things looked so fuzzy but it was a clear day. I thought to myself, "You need to clean this front window." So I did, but things didn't look any better. I leaned over to get my towel out of the door's side pocket. My prescription Transition eyeglasses fell off. I picked them up and just as I started to put them back on, I saw all the dust that had gathered on them overnight. After cleaning them, I laughed at myself, thinking "Now that's a shame. Look at the difference now that I've cleaned my glasses!" So don't be so quick to judge the world around you. It may just be your perspective needs to be cleared like my eyeglasses. For when you change, everything around you changes.

Here's another thing to consider. Maybe you are always tired. Think about your daily schedule. Maybe you are a workaholic as I used to be before I learned to manage my time more strategically to balance my work with leisure. It is not always hard work that drains off your energy, but emotional disengagement as well as emotional upheaval are both unrecognized energy vampires. With those constant unguarded thoughts and negatively entrenched habits, your happiness and peacefulness are much more likely to become troubled. Choose to refocus your thoughts. For as a man (or woman) thinks, so is he (or she).

Keep your heart free from hate. Keep your mind free from worry. Live simply, expect little but give much. Fill your life with love. Scatter sunshine. Forget about yourself and think more often of others.

Do as you would have done unto you. For every day above ground, in my opinion, is the best day ever. Why?

The Best Day Ever

Today, when I awoke, I suddenly realized that this is the best day of my life, ever! There were times when I wondered if I would make it to today; but I did! And because I did I'm going to celebrate!

Today, I'm going to celebrate what an unbelievable life I have:

The relationships,

the accomplishments,

the many blessings,

The opportunities,

and, yes, even the hardships because they have served to make me stronger.

I will go through this day with my head held high, with a happy heart. I will marvel at God's many amazing gifts: the morning dew, the sun, the clouds, the trees, the flowers, that butterfly passing by, the cat sitting on a post, the joyful gait of a puppy walking with its owner and even the rejoicing, ever singing birds. Today, none of these miraculous creations will escape my notice.

Today, I will share my excitement for life with other people. I'll make someone smile. I'll go out of my way to perform an unexpected act of kindness for someone I don't even know.

Today, I'll give a sincere compliment to someone who seems down. I'll tell a child how special he is, and I'll tell someone I love just how deeply I care for them and how much they mean to me.

Today is the day I quit worrying about what I don't have and start being grateful for all the wonderful things God has already given me. I'll remember that to worry is just a waste of time because my faith in God and his Divine Plan ensures everything will be just fine.

Tonight, before I go to bed, I'll go outside and raise my eyes to the heavens. I will stand in awe at the beauty of the stars and the moon, and I will praise God for these magnificent treasures.

As the day ends and I lay my head down on my pillow, I will thank Him for the best day of my life.And I will sleep the sleep of a contented child, excited with expectation because I know that just as today was the best day ever, tomorrow will be too, because my loving Heavenly Father is working everything out for good for me due to my abundant love for Him, just as He promised in Romans 8:28. Therefore, every day is going to be the best day ever!

May I never forget that this life is a gift. I want to enjoy the journey!

Every good and perfect gift is from above, coming down from the Father of the heavenly lights, who does not change like shifting shadows. James 1:17

"Let the rain kiss you. Let the rain beat upon your head with silver liquid drops. Let the rain sing you a lullaby."

Langston Hughes

Humor, like rest and gratitude, is vital to our well being, as noted by the famous poet, Langston Hughes:

"Humor is laughing at what you haven't got when you ought to have it." In other words, look on the bright side. For example many people are unhappy when it rains, but Langston Hughes showed another perspective.

"Like a welcome summer rain, humor may suddenly cleanse and cool the earth, the air and you."

Langston Hughes

Rest is Best

Did you know that our world is so beset by such frenetic activity that rest appears to be a forgotten art? The art of rest and relaxation involves the cessation of work, without exertion, without activity, resulting in the reward of a peaceful ease. Research proves that such a restful peace relieves physical, emotional and mental disturbances, resulting in healing, tranquility and rejuvenation. Making time for downtime Is vital. Just as doctor visits and other self care appoinments, time for rest and relaxation must be made a priority. Taking time to slow down is essential, particularly when you are feeling overburdened, overcommitted, burned out and severely stressed.

In fact, it is proven that rest restores energy and vigor to the human body. Many illnesses are either caused or worsened by the presence of stress. Therefore, just by resting, some of the minor illnesses can be cured instead of the usual tendency of many to take the easy way out through taking a pill. Many benefits are derived from getting a sufficient amount of rest and relaxation. According to research, if you get less than eight hours of sleep a night, it is certainly possible that your productivity, alertness, general health and creativity may be seriously affected. Therefore, it is vital to sleep more than eight hours a night. It is between the seventh and eighth hour that we get almost an hour of rapid eye movement or REM sleep. This is the critical hour when the mind repairs itself and grows new connections. Rest repairs the body, because as we sleep, all the activities of the body slow down, enabling our building cells to perform their recuperative work. As we sleep, nature builds up and repairs the wastes of our body's organisms. Our tired bodies are invigorated by sleep and prepared for the next day's activities. Here are more benefits of sufficient rest and relaxation:

Rest gives us more energy.

Rest is curative:

- ❖ Rest increases blood flow to the muscles

- ❖ Rest decreases muscle tension

- ❖ Rest reduces blood pressure

- ❖ Rest improves and enhances immunity

- ❖ Rest and sufficient sleep slow the rate of breathing, which reduces the need for oxygen

- ❖ Rest increases energy

- ❖ Rest helps increase concentration

- ❖ Rest results in fewer headaches and less pain

- ❖ Rest improves problem solving abilities

- ❖ Rest gives greater efficiency

- ❖ Rest restores us when we are tired

❖ Rest and relaxation improves emotional stability by decreasing anxiety, anger, weeping and frustration

❖ Relaxation gives better sleep

With all these benefits, it behooves us to learn how to rest. Certainly, we are often overworked and overcommitted, with many things on our to do list for the day, such as taking care of our children, going to appointments, paying bills, and so on. There are even times, admittedly, that we end our work day with the intention to rest, yet instead of resting once we get home, we begin doing our housework, gardening, or doing home repairs, completely forgetting to rest. Since a lack of rest could result in headaches, the common cold and stress, among other ailments, we need to consider some alternatives to these varied activities. Have you considered sharing the housework and chores with others in your household? If you live alone, consider portioning out your task load by a 2-3 tasks a day, doing this each day a week, instead of trying to do all 15-20 tasks in one day. Ask for childcare help from family and friends. Also, cancel unimportant appointments, for time to rest is a lifesaver. Not getting enough rest can negatively affect your memory, mood, immune system and your stress level. Moreover, I suggest that we each make rest a priority by:

❖ Listening to some relaxing music

❖ Lying down doing absolutely nothing

❖ Sitting on the patio, deck or in the back yard, just relaxing

❖ Relaxing at the park or beach, watching wildlife and nature

❖ Take a leisurely walk around the neighborhood

❖ Stretching

❖ Doing some yoga or Tai Chi

❖ Sleeping

❖ Try some five minute relaxation techniques that can be practiced any time or place for a

❖ quick refresh: Take some deep breaths while focusing on each time you inhale and exhale. Sit or lie in a comfortable position. Put your hands on your abdomen and as you breathe in, let it expand like a balloon filling with air. As you exhale, slowly let the air out. You should feel your abdomen rising and falling as you breathe.

❖ Try to raise your shoulders up to your ears for 5 seconds, and then let your shoulders drop. One at a time, rotate each shoulder backward 5 to 10 times, and then rotate them together 5 to 10 times.

❖ In a relaxed position, close your eyes and breathe naturally. Think of the number 'one' as you inhale. Continue this for at least five minutes.

Give your mind a break. Relaxation is not just about resting your body. Resting your mind is equally important. If you struggle with constantly worrying or stressing about certain concerns, write them down, then put the list aside for a few days and then revisit it. Sometimes when we give our mind a break from certain thoughts, we return with greater clarity. Also, consider participating in an activity that requires your full attention, such as playing a team sport, like tennis, soccer or basketball. This type of activity can give you a mental break by requiring you to be fully 'in the moment' both physically and mentally, leaving little time to think about your to-do list.

Now as important as learning how to rest is, it is critical to learn how to prepare to rest or sleep by setting a daily regimen. This is very simple to do. Here are a few suggestions to put into practice:

❖ Follow a routine of transitions. Instead of waking up and immediately jumping into the day at high-speed, or vice-versa when going to bed, follow a routine that allows you time to transition from one part of the day into the next. For example, consider waking up 10 minutes earlier and before turning on the TV, radio, computer or cell phone, take the time to do some simple stretches.

❖ Establish a definite time for going to bed and for waking up: avoid sleeping in after unrest

❖ Prepare a comfortable sleeping environment that is not too hot, bright, noisy nor too cold

❖ Either remove or turn off all electronic devices prior to sleeping

❖ Try to relax at least a half hour before going to bed

❖ Here are some things to avoid prior to bedtime:

❖ Avoid eating a heavy meal late at night

❖ Avoid caffeine, alcohol and nicotine within six hours of bedtime

❖ Avoid watching or checking the clock throughout the night

❖ Avoid exercise within four hours of bedtime; it is beneficial to exercise in the middle of the day

Let us realize that both rest, as well as sleep, revitalize and restore our bodies. We should all follow Almighty God's example. In six days, He created, communicated and related, then on the seventh day, God rested. He designed us for productivity, relationship and rest. After all, it is during sleep and rest that there is growth and repair of the tissues in the body. This is also when our energy is conserved and stored. Rest gives us a good start to the day and enables us to be well focussed and more effective in what we think, say and do. Finally, let us remember the True Source of rest:

My soul finds rest in God alone; my slavation comes from Him...Find rest, O my soul, in God alone; my hope comes from Him. – Psalm 62:1, 5

Take time to be still in God's presence. The more hassled you feel, the more you need this sacred space of communion with Him. Breathe slowly and deeply. Relax in His holy Presence. Let His Face shine upon you, for this is how you receive His Peace, which He always offers to each of us. Imagine the pain He feels when we tie ourselves up on ever more anxious knots, ignoring God's gift of Peace. Jesus died a criminal's death to secure this wonderful blessing for each of us who will receive it. Receive it gratefully and hide it in your heart. This Peace is an inner treasure, growing within you as you trust in Him. Therefore, circumstances cannot touch it. Be still, enjoying this holy Peace in His glorious Presence.

As you get out of bed in the morning, be aware of His holy Presence for God is with you. After all, one of Jesus' names is Immanuel, which means God with us. You may not be thinking clearly yet upon awakening, but He is, and He rejoices when you spend time with Him. Otherwise, your early morning thoughts tend anxious ones until you get connected with the Lord. Invite Him into your thoughts by whispering His name in prayer. Suddenly your day brightens and feels more user friendly. Do not let anxiety fill you with dread. Gain confidence knowing that God is with you, for with Him, you face nothing alone. Realize that you and the Lord together can handle anything that occurs. In this you can face the day cheerfully. You cannot dread a day nor a single moment that is vibrant with His Presence.

In the morning, O Lord, You hear my voice; in the morning I lay my requests before You and wait in expectation. –Psalm 5:3

I can do everything through Him Who gives me strength. – Psalm 63:1

Be still, and know that I am God; I will be exalted among the nations, I will be exalted in the earth. –Psalm 46:10

The Lord make His Face shine upon you and be gracious to you; the Lord turn His Face toward you and give you peace. – Numbers 6:25-26

References

Relaxation

http://heartofhealing.net/relaxation-wellness/benefits-of-relaxation

Sleep and Tiredness

http://www.nhs.uk/planners/birthtofive/pages/sleepandtiredness.aspx

Insomniahttp://nhs.uk/Conditions/Insomnia/Pages/Treatment.aspx

Better Sleephttp://www.apshelplink.com

Be One who Tends Your Garden

The winter season in our inner life can be challenging because of its stillness and dormancy as we experience life's setbacks. Yet this season offers valuable lessons and a resource that is in short supply in this world: time for prayer, gratitude, hope, reflection, rest, restoration and quiet. As you read the following passages, may you find support for your journey on the spiritual path. As you read, consider journaling to enable a deeper reflection as you take the time to appreciate the gifts of the winter season.

BE A VICTOR: OVERCOME ADVERSITY

There are many times in life when the unexpected, the unthinkable or even the egregious occurs in a totally unprecedented way, catching you off guard. Instead of losing faith, stop, be still and pray, for it is written in Colossians 4:2, "Devote yourselves to prayer, being watchful and thankful." Every time something derails your plans, desires and intentions, use that as a reminder to communicate with the Lord. There are several benefits to this practice, which, in my opinion, should be part of one's daily regimen.

Talking with God blesses you and strengthens your relationship with Him. Also, when disappointments come, they will not drag you down. In fact, instead of dragging you down, those disappointments are transformed by the Lord for good to those who love Him and are called to serve His purpose. In your relationship with the Lord, this transformation removes the intended sting from the difficult circumstances, making it possible to be joyful even in the midst of adversity. With Him, there is peace beyond human understanding, which is one of the caveats or benefits of having a relationship with Him through accepting the gift of salvation through the incredible sacrifice Jesus Christ made on our behalf.

Begin by practicing this discipline in all the little or large disappointments of daily life. Often, these minor setbacks attempt to draw you away from God's omnipresent presence. However, when you reframe the setbacks as opportunities, you will find that you gain far more than you have lost. It is only after much faith training that you can accept major losses in this positive way. Still, it is possible to gain the perspective of the apostle Paul, who wrote in Philippians 3:7-8: Compared to the surpassing greatness of knowing Jesus Christ, I consider everything I once treasured to be as insignificant as rubbish. In simpler language, my own prayer is:

More of You Lord, less of me

Make me who I am meant to be

You're all I want, all I need

You're my Everything.

Take it all, I surrender.

Be my King. Lord I choose

More of You and less of me.

All to You I completely surrender

All to You my Blessed Savior

I surrender all.

Here's the bottom line from my own experiences. For example, after almost two months of hard labor, my paycheck was not received on time. At first, my emotions went from disappointment to fury then to tearful exasperation, which was increasing my blood pressure. Finally, I sat down and became very quiet. In the stillness, I prayed, read the Word and listened to wise counsel, as well as music that ministered to my weary spirit. I went to sleep trusting God to work it out. The next day, when none of my calls were answered by a particular person, I made a call to a more reliable contact. I learned that an internal file error was made that caused an egregious delay in being paid since my bank returned the improperly noted deposit upon receipt. In meeting the key people to discuss the next steps, the fact was revealed that the department had indeed received my appropriately filed update document but somehow used the deleted bank account for the automatic deposit. I made the necessary correction by filing the correct required information again and asked the personnel to call me when my money finally arrived in their office so that I can be called for immediate retrieval. Through it all, I learned to communicate effectively, deal only with the facts, get the desired results, talk with the bank as well as the particular department, call creditors to reschedule payments, and do it all in a calm demeanor without having to go to the extremes of filing a legal claim. All the way there and en route home, I continued to praise God for His calming, peaceful Presence. Surely God will get the glory for the resulting testimony when all this is resolved. Meanwhile, I will trust in the Lord with all my heart, and I will not lean on my own understanding. In all my ways, I will acknowledge Him and He will make my paths straight, according to the promises of Proverbs 3:5-6.

So, whenever things seem to be going wrong, trust God. When your life feels increasingly out of control, thank Me. These are supernatural responses, and they can lift you above your circumstances. If you do what comes naturally in the face of difficulties, you may fall prey to negativism. Even a few complaints can set you on a path that is a downward spiral, by darkening your perspective and mind-set. With this attitude controlling you, complaints flow more and more readily from your mouth. Each one moves you steadily down the slippery spiral. The lower you go, the faster you slide; but it is still possible to apply brakes. Cry out to Me in My Name! Affirm your trust in Me, regardless of how you feel. Thank Me for everything, though this seems unnatural—even irrational. Gradually you will begin to ascend, recovering your lost ground.

When you are back on ground level, you can face your circumstances from a humble perspective. If you choose supernatural responses this time—trusting and thanking Me—you will experience My unfathomable Peace.

But I trust in your unfailing love; my heart rejoices in your salvation.

—Psalm 13:5

Always giving thanks to God the Father for everything, in the name of our Lord Jesus Christ.

—Ephesians 5:20

So, expect to encounter adversity in your life. Remember that we live in a fallen world. Stop trying to find a way to circumvent difficulties to make life easier. The key problem with an easy life is that it masks your need for the Lord. When people choose to become a Christian, God infuses His life into believers, and empowers them to live on a supernatural level with His power by depending on Him. This reminds me of Don Moen's uplifting hymn that I learned in choir rehearsal, "Be Strong and Take Courage:"

Be strong and take courage, do not fear or be dismayed

For the Lord will go before you and His light will show the way

Be strong and take courage, do not fear or be dismayed

For The One Who lives within you will be strong in you today.

Why don't you give Him all of your fears

Why don't you let Him wipe all of your tears

He knows, He's been through pain before

And He knows all that you've been looking for…

Nothing can take you out of His hand

Nothing can face you that you can't command

I know that you will always be

In His love, in His power, you will be free!....

So, realize confidently that nothing takes God by surprise. In order to have a testimony, (that is, an experience to share how God has brought you through a difficulty), one must have a test. After all, it is in the test that patience, strength, faith and perseverance are developed. God will not allow circumstances to overwhelm you as long as you look to Him. Just hang in there, trusting Him to bring you through. He will help you cope with whatever the moment or situation presents. Collaborating with God brings blessings that far outweigh all troubles. Remain aware of His holy Presence for it contains joy that can endure all eventualities. Reflect on Psalm 23:1-4:

"The Lord is my Shepherd; I shall not want. He makes me to lie down in green pastures; He leads me beside the still waters. He restores my soul; He leads me in the paths of righteousness for His name's sake. Yes, though I walk through the valley of the shadow of death, I will fear no evil; for You are with me; Your rod and Your staff, they comfort me."

Take courage in the words of Second Corinthians 4:16-17: "Therefore we do not lose heart. Though outwardly we are wasting away, yet inwardly we are being renewed day by day. For our light and momentary troubles are achieving for us an eternal glory that far outweighs them all."

Therefore, anticipate coming face to face with life's impossibilities, situations that are totally beyond your ability to handle them. The awareness of your inadequacy is precisely the perfect place to encounter God's glory and power at its utmost as you turn to Him for help, wisdom and guidance. When you see these armies of problems marching toward you, cry out to the Lord! Allow Him to fight for you and watch Him work on your behalf. That is what He is here for. You were never expected to do it all on your own. As the famed Allstate commercial says, "Put yourself in our hands." Put yourself in God's capable hands as you rest in the shadow of His Almighty Presence. Be encouraged. Just remember the words of John Mason Neale, 1862, as noted in the following poem, and Psalm 91:1, "He who dwells in the shelter of the Most High will rest in the shadow of the Almighty."

Christian, do you struggle on the battleground,

'gainst the powers of darkness closing in around?

Christian, rise, take armor, soldier of the cross;

For the sake of Jesus count your gain but loss.

Christian, do you battle Satan' power within,

All his striving, luring, tempting you to sin?

Christian, do not tremble, do not be downcast;

Arm yourself for battle, watch and pray and fast.

Christian, do you wrestle those who taunt and claim,

"Why keep fast and vigil? Prayer is said in vain!"

Christian, answer boldly: "While I breathe I pray!"

Peace shall follow battle, night shall end in day.

May encouragement strengthen you as I close this chapter with the following words by the singing group, Casting Crowns:

I was sure by now God, You would have reached down and wiped our tears away….As the thunder rolls, I barely hear Your whisper through the rain, saying "I'm with you," and as Your mercy falls, I raise my hands and praise the God Who gives and takes away…I remember when I stumbled in the win. You heard my cry to You and You raised me up again. My strength is almost gone. How can I carry on if I can't find You? But as the thunder rolls, I will praise You in this storm and I will lift my hands, for You are who You are, no matter where I am and every tear I've cried, You hold in Your hand. You never left my side and though my heart is torn, I will praise You in this storm.

Now from Psalm 121:1-8, be comforted: *I lift up my eyes to the hills - where does my help come from? My help comes from the Lord, The Maker of heaven and earth. He will not let your foot slip: He who watches over you will not slumber; indeed, He who watches over Israel will neither slumber nor sleep. The Lord watches over you: the Lord is your shade at your right hand; the sun will not harm you bye day, nor the moon by night. The Lord will keep you from all harm – He will watch over your life; the Lord will watch over your coming and going both now and forevermore.*

Therefore, no matter what, keep praising God for He has you safely in the palm of His hand.

BE ONE WHO DEALS WITH THE D'S: DISAPPOINTMENT AND DISCOURAGEMENT

Have you ever had your share of heartbreaks, disappointments, unanswered prayers, dashed hopes or unrealized desires? Although I am strong woman of faith who loves God emphatically, there have been challenging times in my life where I prayed and believed for certain things that surely were God's will, yet did not get fulfilled or answered. I know the Lord has only the best plans for my life. He deeply cares about me, my desires, always listening to me, helping me at all times, and interceding on my behalf. According to Jeremiah 29:11-13, *"For I know the plans I have for you," declares the Lord, "plans to prosper you and not to harm you, plans to give you hope and a future. Then you will call upon me and come and pray to me, and I will listen to you. You will seek Me and find Me when you seek Me with all your heart."* Admittedly, even I have wondered about His silence regarding unanswered prayers, pain and devastating disappointments. Sometimes my hope has all but died as I've asked for better situations in life instead of all the lemon juice that seems to rain so frequently on me. Why did He let me get my hopes up so high if He knew it was not going to happen, or was not going to happen in that exact way or at that particular time? Faith is at times difficult to fathom in these types of trying situations when we ask, "Why me? Why do bad things happen?" We all may want better circumstances, but even we must realize that God is using our circumstances to make us better. This is why we have these seasons of life.

I am reminded of the time when Arthur Ashe, the famous Wimbledon legend, was dying of AIDS. He contracted AIDS in 1983 during a heart surgery through infected blood that he received during the operation. Many of his fans wrote him letters from all around the world. Some asked him, "Why does God have to select you for such a bad disease?" I was silenced and awed by his humble reply:

"The world over – 50 million children start playing tennis; 5 million learn to play tennis; 500,000 learn professional tennis; 50,000 come to the tennis circuit; 5,000 reach the grand slam; 50 players reach Wimbledon; 4 go to the semifinals; 2 go to the finals. When I was holding a cup, I never asked God "Why me? And today in pain, I should not be asking God, 'Why me?' Therefore, happiness keep you sweet. Trials keep you strong. Sorrow keeps you human."

We all are human. We all deal with trying times and challenging emotions. Still, the fact is that God is faithful. He is still good all the time. All the time, God is good to us, loving us far more than we know. Despite our fickle feelings, let us reconcile the Truth for the Word clarifies:

God's plans for us are wonderful.Jeremiah 29:11-13

God is for us.Romans 8:31

He makes All things work for our good.Romans 8:28

Herein we see the truth, so let us use the following strategies to speak to our hearts and ease the heartaches of dealing with the D's, otherwise known as disappointments and discouragement. Let the truth set us free indeed.

Let us be thankful to God.

In First Thessalonians 5:16-18, we are instructed, "*Be joyful always; pray continually; give thanks in all circumstances, for this is God's will for you in Christ Jesus.*" When the hard blows of not getting what you desire pierces your spirit, that is a strong indication that whatever that thing was, it had mighty large hold on you. When you are believing God for something, it had the ability or propensity to overtake your thoughts, thinking "this is going to make life so much better," making you completely forget all the many things God has already blessed

159

you with. On the other hand, when you begin meditating on all that God has done for you, such as saving your life, for starters, then you realize that what you were hoping and wishing for is put into its proper perspective. He is our Source, our true Joy, and our Hope. So I imagine that I must look like a whiny toddler to the Lord, laying out my laundry list of bossy demands: "Lord, all I really want is some much needed relief from all these circumstances that are stressing me out, and while You're at it, I want some assurance that this stuff will never happen again, oh and while You're listening, Lord, will You please answer my questions (as I unfurl this list that's a mile long) and please give me a road map detailing just like my GPS exactly what's going to happen next and when, pretty please? Hey God, why are You laughing?" Even I am giggling as I look at how ridiculous this looks in writing. You know what? In spite of all the things I am dealing with, none of them are bigger than our heavenly Father God, so what am I worried about? What are you worried about? Let us agree to rest and trust God in the midst of our life storms. Let us lean and totally rely on Him for He is the Artist, the Potter, our Creator and the True Transformer. Surely whatever is happening, He will turn around for our good, according to Romans 8:28, as quoted earlier. Let us also remember and realize that things are not always the way they appear, for 2 Corinthians 5:7 enlightens us that *"We live by faith, not by sight."*

Moreover, realize the truth of Ephesians 2:10 and reflect: *For we are God's workmanship, created in Christ Jesus to do good works, which God prepared in advance for us to do.* In reading Rick Warren's book, "The Purpose Driven Life," I remember and realize that this life is not "poor little me." Absolutely not! This life is about serving others, learning, growing more in Christ's likeness and character, and being blessed to be a blessing. That diamond making process that was discussed in an earlier chapter is no walk in the park. From much pain, comes much beauty, all in the Lord's perfect timing. I think of the delay that Abraham and Sarah experienced, both in their ultra senior years, and told by the Lord that Sarah would give birth. Imagine that: in your 90's or even 100 years old, well past the usual childbearing years! Yet that is exactly what happened: Sarah gave birth to Isaac, a name which means laughter, for Sarah laughed when she heard she would give birth. Maybe you are brokenhearted over a breakup. Well, the Lord may be working behind the scenes preparing special someone for you who is the perfect fit, not only for you, but for what the Lord intends for both of your lives. If it's a financial setback, perhaps the Lord has a better plan for your financial increase, or even a better timing. Maybe even how you responded with key personnel will be used to divine advantage on your behalf. Just know that He has our best interests at heart.

Realize that His perfect timing has its perfect purpose. I watched a chef make a showstopper of a cake on one of these wonderful cooking shows. He had all the ingredients laid out, and each of the ingredients had to be the best for he stressed that quality comes from the right ingredients, the right timing and the right temperature; the order things were put into the mixer had to be just right; the right pan had to be properly prepared; the best temperature was set, and the timer had to be exact so that the cake would not bake a second too soon nor a minute too long. The cake had to cool so that the frosting wouldn't melt all over the place. All the frosting and fancy add ons had to be set in place just right, and the dish that the cake was plated on was ornately decorated. The finished presentation looked so lovely, just picture perfect. When they sliced that cake, I could almost taste it through the television screen! That cake is just like us. God puts each of us in a circle of opportunity, and gets everything just right to prepare us for what we are here to do. He allows things to happen to fine tune us, then uses us to touch the lives of those in that circle while He sharpens us, prunes us, weeds out all the ugliness in our hearts and shapes us to be more fulfilling in His overall plan for our lives. After all is said and done, we are His masterpiece, full of wonderful testimonies that benefit all those who hear them. I remember the words of Ecclesiastes 3, where Solomon declares that everything has its season. So who am I to moan and groan, asking "Why me?" Forgive me, Lord, for running my mouth and trying to run this life You've given me. Instead, let there be more of You, and far less of me.

Therefore, let us resolve to **Trust in the Lord:**

Trust in the Lord with all your heart, and do not lean on your own understanding. In all your ways, acknowledge Him and He will make your paths straight. –Proverbs 3:5-6

In an interview called the "Why Me Story" on YouTube, I listened intently as Kris Kristofferson shared the story behind his song, "Why Me Lord?" He said that he heard Larry Gatlin sing this song in church. Kris had been invited to attend this church after doing a benefit for Dottie West. He was so moved by what happened there that during the prayer, while everybody had their heads bowed down, he heard Jimmy the preacher say something like, "If anyone does not know Jesus Christ, raise your hand." Well, he had no intention of raising his hand since he didn't want anyone to see him doing that. Next thing he knew, he felt his hand go up. Then he heard the preacher say something like, "If you want to know Jesus, come down front." Now Kris had no intention of moving from his seat, yet next thing he knew, he was walking down front with the rest of the people in the aisle. Kris said that he really does not know what the preacher said next, but after he knelt down and heard the preacher praying, he felt such a relief and release that he had never felt before as he accepted Jesus Christ into his heart. It was truly life changing, as I can attest from my own personal experience of receiving Christ as my Savior. So, may the lyrics of this Kris Kristofferson song, sung by Johnny Cash and so many others, minister to each of us, for these words can certainly speak to all of our hearts.

Why me Lord? What have I ever done to deserve

Even one of the pleasures I've known?

Tell me Lord? What did I ever do that was worth

Love from You and the kindness You've shown?

LIVE SUNNY SIDE UP!

Lord, help me, Jesus
I've wasted it so
Help me Jesus
I know what I am.

Now that I know
That I've needed You so
Help me Jesus
My soul's in Your hand.

Try me Lord, if You think there's a way
That I can try to repay all I've taken from You
Maybe Lord, I could show someone else
What I've been through myself
On my way back to You.

Lord, help me, Jesus
I've wasted it so
Help me Jesus
I know what I am.

Now that I know
That I've needed You so
Help me Jesus
My soul's in Your hand
Jesus, my soul's in Your hand.

BE TRANSFORMED BY A RENEWED MIND

A CHANGED MIND, A CHANGED LIFE

"Every new beginning comes from some other beginnings' end."
—*Semisonic*

"I appeal to you therefore, brothers, by the mercies of God, to present your bodies as a living sacrifice, holy and acceptable to God, which is your spiritual worship. [2] *Do not be conformed to this world, but be transformed by the renewal of your mind, that by testing you may discern what is the will of God, what is good and acceptable and perfect."* — Romans 12:1-2

It is vital to remember that when something big changes our lives, it simply means something better is coming. As something moves out, something must be coming in to replace it for that is God's divine design. Therefore, instead of resisting rebelliously to prevent the inevitable changes from occurring, or overreacting when those changes finally occur, just relax and choose to be part of the process. Trust the Lord, the Renewer and Transformer, instead of ranting, "We've done it this way for 40 years." Stop relying on your limited human understanding. Realize that just like the seasons change from warm to cold, from summer to winter, life changes must also occur, for this is a necessary part of growth. Grow in His Presence and promises, for He is faithful to complete the work He began in each of us. Have faith in God and know that any changes He brings about are all for good. His plans are to help you, not to harm you. He promised to give you hope and a good future in Jeremiah 29:11. So realize that something more magnificent is coming your way and get ready for it!

Now, let's look more closely at the earlier scripture mentioned from Romans 12:1-2. When you focus on the phrase in Romans 12:2, "by the renewal of your mind," that is a clear indication that our minds are not to stay the same as they were before Christ entered our lives. The scripture goes on to say," Do not be conformed to this world, but be transformed by the renewal of your mind, that by testing you may discern what is the will of God, what is good and acceptable and perfect." Remember, we are perfectly useless as Christ-exalting Christians if all we do is to do what everyone else in the world is doing. *Non*conformity, i.e. do **not** be conformed to this world. After all, we are to be, by design, peculiarly different, as we like a lighthouse on a hill shine brightly for God's glory. Just because everyone else is fighting and full of rage does not mean that we should be doing the same. In fact, we should be doing the opposite. I am pointing this out to make the point that the *non*conformity to the world does not primarily mean the external avoidance of worldly behaviors. Although that is included, you can avoid all kinds of worldly behaviors and still *not* be transformed. The Bible says of Moses after spending time with the Lord in the mountain, preparing the Ten Commandments, *"His face shown like the sun, and his clothes became white as light!"* Something noticeable happens to us spiritually, morally and mentally, first on the inside, as we grow more in the Lord's likeness. Our thinking is changed, what we choose to talk about is changed, habits are changed, and lifestyle is changed as He uses His process of transformation in our lives; it starts on the inside. and then, later at the resurrection, it will show on the outside. This is the triumphant power and metamorphosis brought about by God's Holy Spirit at work in us, through our faith in Jesus Christ, our Lord, Savior and Treasure. This is a blood-bought, Spirit wrought change from the inside out. This is a spiritual act of worship and it displays that Christ is far more worthy, high above the worth of the world. So Jesus says of us, in Matthew 13:43, at the resurrection: *"Then the righteous will shine like the sun in the kingdom of their Father."*

Now, by the "renewing of the mind," the Bible is referring to having a changed mindset, a changed spirit, a new attitude and an improved viewpoint, in full acceptance of the supremacy of the Most High God, Who is infinitely more worthy of all of our praise that we will ever be, make or achieve on our own without Christ.

In Ephesians 4:17–18, the Bible clarifies further, *"You must no longer walk as the Gentiles do, in the futility of their* minds. *They are darkened in their* understanding, *alienated from the life of God because of the* ignorance *that is in them, due to their hardness of heart."* The Apostle Paul's inspired explanation penetrates beneath the words "futile mind" and the "darkened understanding" and the *"willful ignorance,"* by clarifying that this darkness of the mind is all rooted in *"the hardness of their heart."* Herein is the deepest disease, infecting everything else. The bottom line is that our deep mental suppression of liberating gospel truth is rooted in our hardness of heart. Our hard hearts will not submit to the supremacy of Christ, and therefore our blind minds cannot see the supremacy of Christ without His Holy Spirit's enlightenment.

Now, the remedy is that the Holy Spirit renews the mind, in order for us and obey Romans 12:2, *"Be transformed in the renewal of your mind."* First, the Holy Spirit is our Source of renewal, as noted in Titus 3:5 where Paul says, *"God saved us, not because of works done by us in righteousness, but according to his own mercy, by the washing of regeneration and* **renewal of the Holy Spirit.***"* Clearly, the Holy Spirit renews the mind. It is first and decisively His work. We are totally dependent on Him. Our efforts follow his initiatives and enablings.

Moreover, in 2 Corinthians 3:18 is a further clarification of this process: *"And we all, with unveiled face,* beholding the glory of the Lord, *are being transformed into the same image from one degree of glory to another. For this comes from the Lord who is the Spirit."* Therefore, the Holy Spirit "transforms" us into the image of Jesus Christ, the God-exalting Son of God. He enables us to *"behold the glory of the Lord."* This is how the mind is renewed — by steadfastly gazing at the glories of Christ for what they really are, as He transforms us from the outside in and from the inside out. He must work from the outside in by exposes the mind to Christ-exalting truth by leading us to hear the Gospel, to read the Bible, to study the writings of Christ-exalting men and women, and cause us to meditate on the perfection of Christ. This is exactly what our lowly enemy does not want us to do, as previously mentioned from the Screwtape Letters, and also according to 2 Corinthians 4:4, "The god of this world [Satan] has blinded the *minds* of the unbelievers, to keep them from *seeing the light of the gospel of the glory of Christ*,"because to see the glory of Christ will renew the mind, and transform the life and produce a life of unending worship.

Additionally, the Holy Spirit must work from the inside out, breaking the hard heart that blinds and corrupts the mind so that the Gospel Truth would not be despised and rejected. Transforming the mind, therefore, enables a person to accept, embrace and worship Jesus Christ as Lord and Savior, gaining eternal life.

Let us all pray that the Holy Spirit will renew all minds, so that each of us may desire and approve the will of God, so that all of our lives will become full of worship to the glory of Christ.

May the mind of Christ, my Savior live in me from day to day,

By His love and power controlling all I do and say.

May the Word of God dwell richly in my heart from hour to hour,

So that all may see I triumph only through His power.

May the peace of God my Father rule my life in everything,

That I may be calm to comfort the sick and sorrowing.

May the love of Jesus fill me as the waters fill the sea;

Him exalting, self abasing, for this is victory.

May I run the race before me, strong and brave to face the foe,

Looking only unto Jesus as I onward go.

May His beauty rest upon me, as I seek the lost to win,

And may they forget the channel, seeing only Him.

Kate Wilkenson

BE A FRIEND OF CHANGE

Change is inevitable. Nothing stays the same, so why not get prepared for change to happen? Be a participant in the change, and growth will follow. Refuse to change, and difficulties will follow, for you are blocking God's promotion to your next level of purpose.

Life seems easiest when you are young and unobligated to take care of any responsibilities. This is why it is essential that parents teach responsibilities to their children so that the discipline of taking care of a pet, doing certain chores or getting their homework done on time will already be well established in their thinking and lifestyle choices. Once you get older, trials and difficulties begin to shape your experiences and develop your wisdom. So choose wisely.

Failures and mistakes are the steppingstones to deeper growth. Learn the lessons from those mistakes and failures, and move on with your life.

Lessons learned:

Wisdom is gained through experiences along the journey.

Things happen to guide you towards your destiny.

Blind trust in the Lord, following God's plan, causes time to fly by faster than you realize.

Don't lament about the past. Learn the lessons, do the work and grow.

Training is good but instinct is mandatory: one must know how to do what is required and why to do what is essential.

A lion raised in captivity knows nothing about how to live in the wild.

We each need to be with people who have our same rhythm; surround yourself with those who are likeminded in spirit, focus, perspective and vision.

Creativity seeks its own level. Don't apologize for being peculiarly different.

When it's time to leave the familiar to matriculate to your next level of growth, you must either leave on your own, or God will push you out, kicking and screaming. Which way do you often choose?

Nobody drifts toward discipline, wisdom, or humility. It is a daily pursuit.

Choose the values that bring you joy and are pleasing to God.

BE PLEASING TO GOD WITH YOUR CHOICES

Now this last point brings to mind a biography I read about. The title, "Empty Mansions" intrigued me during the television commercial, so I chose to keep watching and listening. I learned about a quiet reclusive heiress, who chose to live in a hospital for over twenty years, leaving her several mansions empty. Although she was exorbitantly wealthy, she was not living it up as one would expect. Who was this mysterious woman and what was her story? What choices did she make that brought joy and pleased God?

Her name was Huguette Clark. A prolific artist and musician, her paintings were exhibited in Washington, D.C.'s Corcoran Gallery of Art. She was the youngest daughter of William A. Clark, a United States Senator for the state of Montana and an industrialist. Mr. Clark was a businessman known for his immense wealth in copper mining and railroads. Upon his death in 1925, Ms. Clark and her mother moved from their 962 Fifth Avenue mansion on the Upper East Side of Manhattan, New York to a twelfth floor apartment located at 907 Fifth Avenue, and while there, she later purchased the entire eighth floor of the building they resided in.

Although commonly presumed dead by her employees, in fact, Ms. Clark was quite alive. Yet throughout her life, she simply preferred to live a quiet, unobtrusive life within tightly controlled surroundings, after spending her childhood and young adulthood as a famed, jewel bedecked heiress to an immense copper fortune. Therefore, Ms. Clark chose not to live in any of her homes. All told, she owned a mesa estate in Santa Barbara, California, along with a New Canaan, Connecticut mansion that had not been occupied since its purchase in 1951, and over forty rooms in a grand Fifth Avenue building that contained three apartments. She named the Santa Barbara estate the Andree Clark Bird Refuge, in memory of her late sister, who dies of meningitis.

Through the years, Huguette developed a pronounced distrust of her family and all outsiders. She believed they all were after her money. Consequently, all of her conversations were conducted in French in order to prevent others from understanding the discussions, since it was highly unlikely that others would be well versed in that language. Married and divorced, she was decidedly sequestered in a New York hospital room, after suffering from illness. By choice, Huguette, at 103 years of age, had not been to any of her homes in over twenty years. Her caretakers of three of the properties had never met their employer, which is why the famed Bill Dedman and Paul Newell book was entitled "Empty Mansions." Still, all of the properties and their extensive grounds were meticulously maintained. Despite her air of mystery, she was a caring philanthropist who left most of her more than 300 million dollars to charity after a court fight with her distant relatives, who along with some of her employees, attorney and accountant, received a set amount. However, the bulk of the substantial remainder of funds, along with the gift of her Santa Barbara estate, went to the arts, while her apartments were sold for a handsome sum. While alive, it was said by a paralegal that she also gave lavish gifts to Wallace Bock's law firm, including a gift of $1.5 million to build a bomb shelter in an Israeli settlement in the West Bank near his daughters. Apparently, Ms. Clark chose to think more of others, by sharing her wealth, rather than think only of herself, and that is to be commended.

There is also a historical account in the Bible about a man named Nehemiah and a group of likeminded men? Together, they successfully rebuilt the walls of Jerusalem in only 52 days. These walls had previously been destroyed and left in a pile of rubble for numerous years. This major feat of rebuilding the walls was achieved despite severe harassment and vicious threats by enemies from all around. Because of the ongoing attacks, each builder had to rebuild the wall by holding a sword in one hand and a tool in the other. This was the only way they could work together successfully as a team to get the job done while protecting themselves, for they had to do both simultaneously at a great price. Yet they chose to do so, pleasing God in the process, doing what was necessary to get the job done for God's glory.

Similarly, our lives sometimes are like the walls of Jerusalem, fallen and crumbled into a pile of rubble, with us on top of the heap, under spiritual attack. Recognize that it is time to rebuild and seek those who are allies, like Nehemiah and the men of his generation, to help rebuild our lives. This is no easy task, yet anything worthwhile is worthy of the time and effort required to accomplish it. With prayer and the right support, we too can rise up from the rubble and give God the glory.

_____

_____

_____

_____

_____

_____

Be Sure to Take Time

Take time to think:

it is the source of great ideas.

Take time to read:

it is the foundation of wisdom.

Take time to joke and play:

it is the secret of staying young.

Take time to be quiet:

it is the opportunity to hear God.

Take time to pray:

it is the greatest power on earth.

Take time to see others' needs:

it is the opportunity to help others.

Take time to love and be loved:

it is God's greatest gift.

Take time to praise God: It is the road to worship.

Take time to laugh:

it is the music of the soul.

Take time to be friendly:

it is the pathway to building a community.

Take time to dream:

it is what the future is made of.

Take time to be real:

it is the gift you bring to the world around you. –Vicki Evans

Appreciate time, realizing the gift it truly is. Time is priceless. It offers us a wealth

of opportunity. As the seasons pass so consistently, time comes and goes. We go

through each day in a time zone given freely to us by the Lord who watches over us

day in and day out. Of all the seasons, winter tends to be the most reflective, as

the colder weather slows us down in ways that, in my opinion, tend to be less likely

due to the busier pace of life. I believe that winter offers us many valuable lessons.

However, the winter I am speaking of is not constrained by any calendar. This

winter is a choice, a decision that one makes to be still and grow within. The time

for rest and renewal can happen at any time of the year. I choose to have some

daily time for winter for at least five minutes a day for I function best when I have

time to rest my mind, my body and my spirit. For as Sydney J. Harris quoted, "The

time to relax is when you don't have time for it."

These are the reasons that I believe rest is best. Having time for reflection and renewal are in very short supply in this world. Our hectic lives drive us constantly to be extremely busy, frenetically pushing ourselves at times to risky limits without sufficient rest as we strive to be productive. The frenzy is maddening. It is up to each of us to prioritize our lives in such a way that we have stillness and solitude in each day's merry go round of activity. Take time to slow things down, for it is in the quiet, restful stillness that I find rejuvenation, creativity and life enrichment. No matter where we are, each of us can stop, rest, appreciate and explore the vast richness of our inner lives. Stop for a moment. Take time to feel your pulse, rhythmically beating like a drum, realizing that God is providing every heartbeat, every breath, every ability you have. Think about all the blessings in your life. Journal as you count your blessings. Think about the events and the people who have made a positive difference in your life. Notice the beginnings and endings of different seasons in your life, and be grateful for what you have overcome. Pay attention to areas of your life in which there is room to grow, goals to work towards, dreams to fulfill, and goals that have been achieved. Take time to look outside. Take a walk outside and listen to nature. Just think: "Today is the very first day of the rest of my life," as you read this anonymous poem by the same title.

This is the Beginning of a New Day.

I Can Waste It ... or Use It For Good.

But What I Do Today is Important,

Because I am Exchanging a Day of My Life For It.

When Tomorrow Comes, This Day Will Be Gone Forever,

Leaving in It's Place Something That I Have Traded For It.

I Want It to Be Gain and Not Loss, Good and Not Evil,

Success and Not Failure, in Order That I Not Regret the Price I Have Paid For It.

I Will Give 100% of Myself Just For Today, For You Never Fail

Until You Stop Trying.

I Will Be the Kind of Person I have Always Wanted To Be ...

I Have Been Given This Day to Use as I Will.

Reading this anonymous poem, we should realize that each day we are gifted with new mercies, new grace, new favor, new opportunities to turn things around for the best. So this is why each day is the very first day of the rest of my life. Therefore, be grateful for this precious gift, and choose to use it wisely to be a blessing.

When I dare to be powerful — to use my strength in the service of my vision, then it becomes less and less important whether I am afraid.— Audre Lorde

BE AWARE THAT YOUR MIND MATTERS

Life is a series of choices. Those choices are governed by our thinking. We need to take time to think selectively. Why?

"Watch your thoughts for they become words.

 Watch your words for they become actions.

 Watch your actions for they become habits.

 Watch your habits for they become your character.

 And watch your character for it becomes your destiny.

 What we think, we become."

Quote from Margaret Thatcher, also often attributed to Frank Outlaw and Mahatma Ghandi.

These quoted words articulate the true significance that our thought lives have on our futures, and the incredible impact these thoughts have on our life journeys. The profundity of this reality is infinite. During some quiet thinking, I began to realize that my thoughts are contagious, either positively or negatively. I choose therefore to positively impact my life and those around me with the abundance of beauty and positivity that become possible by the thoughts I choose to think. God's Word instructs me to do this, to choose carefully the thoughts I think. The very thoughts I allow to circulate in my mind must be selectively chosen prior to being focused upon, for thoughts are a freeway or gateway to manifestations in the physical realm.

 Every thought has an agenda, and develops a habit. Habits generally take 21 days to develop, from thinking and doing something over and over and over again. We each must be the Director of our Thought Freeway, and filter what we think with at least three foci, much in the same way as we should filter what we say: Is is true?; Is it necessary? Is it beneficial?

Simply put, each thought shapes my purpose and philosophy of life, and prompts me to move in a particular direction, just like when we drive. As we sit behind the steering wheel of the car, each of us guides the way the car will go, either left or right, forward or backward, slow or fast, even to turn the car on or off. So, decide to filter your thoughts with truth. Your thoughts affect your mind, your feelings, your words, your actions, and your character. Your character shapes your destiny in this journey called life. Some of the scriptures that clarify this point are:

For as he underline thinks within himself, so he is. Proverbs 23:7

Set your mind on things above, not on the things that are on earth. Colossians 3:2

This book of the Law shall not depart from your mouth, but you shall meditate on it day and night, so that you may be careful to do according to all that is written in it; for then you will make your way prosperous, and then you will have success. Joshua 1:8

Finally brethren, whatever is true, whatever is honorable, whatever is right, whatever is pure, whatever is lovely, whatever is of good repute, if there is any excellence and if anything worthy of praise, dwell on these things. Philippians 3:8

For the word of God is living and active and sharper than any two-edged sword, and piercing as far as the division of soul and spirit, of both joints and marrow, and able to judge the thoughts and intentions of the heart. Hebrews 4:12

By thinking and making the wisest decisions, we stand poised to live the happiest life possible, just as God planned and stated for us in

John 10:10: *I came that you may have life, and life more abundantly.*

Yet that abundant life begins by focussing on Christ instead of on the various distractions that can suffocate your purpose. *"For as he thinks within himself, so he is."* Proverbs 23:7

Let us think wholesome thoughts and we will positively become wholesome, with good habits, full of vitality. As the mind goes, the body will follow. I have seen this in my personal life. When I focussed on worry, pain, misery, others' expectations of me, negativity and workaholic tendencies, my health suffered with migraines, weight gain, sleeplessness, constant confusion, frustration, feeling like I was consumed in an endless spinning vortex, significantly less creativity and decreased work productivity. When I changed my mind and thoughts to focus on Christ and positive thoughts, my health was transformed. I went from being 178 pounds to losing 18 pounds, my hair grew, my skin, nails and sleep improved. I became more productive in my work, as well as becoming more creative by gaining and maintaining a well balanced, healthy lifestyle. Changing your mind can change your life.

All Positive Changes First Occur in the Mind
Written by Alex Duarte

I am your greatest helper. I can push you to success or I can be your worst enemy, and I can tear you down to failure. Yet I am under your complete control. Half of the things that you do, you can turn over to me and I will do them automatically and efficiently. I am not a machine, yet I work with the precision of a machine and the intelligence of a man or a woman. If you take me and are firm with me and you discipline me, I will lay the world at your feet. But if you go easy with me, I will destroy you. Who am I? Ladies and gentlemen, I am your habits. I am your good habits and I can push you on to success, or I am your bad habits and I can tear you down to failure.

Every human life tends to follow a timeline in which each of us makes certain key decisions within the same periods of time. Although life is a mysterious journey, we each must rise to the challenge to seek, find and grow in order to make the unique choices that are healthiest for us and those whose lives we impact daily. In that, we fulfill our divine purpose, as noted below.

My Affirmation

I am aware of the fullness of my being, and I am no longer constrained by habits, behaviors, the past, nor conditions which limit me. I am in step with my Lord and Savior, Jesus Christ, and I choose to see God in every person, place and evidence of His creation. I live in God's embrace, and I am fully aware of Him in me, as I live, move and have my being. Everything I am, do and have simply reveals more of God. I am ever thankful for His Holy Presence, Power, Grace, Mercy and Faithfulness. Thanks and more thanks I will always give to my heavenly Father, God, who is the same, yesterday, today and tomorrow, Ever Present, Ever Omniscient, Ever Sovereign. I adore You, Lord. All I am, and all I ever shall be, I owe to You.

The Center of My Joy

Written by Richard Smallwood

Jesus, You're the center of my joy. All that's good and perfect comes from You. You're the heart of my contentment, Hope for all I do. Jesus, You're the center of my joy!

When I've lost my direction, You're the compass for my way.

You're the fire and light when nights are long and cold.

In sadness, You are the laughter that shatters all my fears.

When I'm alone, Your hand is there to hold.

Jesus, You're the center of my joy. All that's good and perfect comes from You. You're the heart of my contentment, Hope for all I do. Jesus, You're the center of my joy!

You are why I find pleasure in the simple things in life.

You're the music in the meadows and the streams.

The voices of the children, my family and my home,

You're the Source and Finish of my highest dreams.

Jesus, You're the center of my joy. All that's good and perfect comes from You. You're the heart of my contentment, Hope for all I do. Jesus, You're the center of my joy, joy, of my joy!

You have made known to me the path of life; You will fill me with joy in Your Presence, with eternal pleasures at your right hand. - Psalm 16:11

One thing is certain. We need to realize that life is best digested in small, gradual doses. If we were to let reality rush in on us all at once each day, we would be in a constant state of drowning. That said, choose to step back and spend some quiet, prayerful time to meditate on the Word at the beginning and end of each day. As a result, because of the quiet reflection, an occasional epiphany or Aha moment may be experienced to deepen your growth. Now please understand, I am not talking about religion. I am talking about the benefits of having a relationship with Jesus Christ.

This spirituality, as some call it, is a Decision, a choice to look at life through a different lens. This new lens sees possibilities rather than liabilities, and realize that we are all connected in some essential way and here on earth for a reason. After all, our greatest power in life is to choose, as I learned many years ago when I read, "Your Greatest Power" and "Your Word is Your Wand" by Florence Scovel Shin, from which I share three of her often quoted affirmations:

"I am as necessary to God as He is to me, for I am the channel to bring His plan to pass."

"The Christ in me is risen, I now fulfill my destiny."

"I do not limit God by seeing limitation in myself. With God all things are possible."

I am a Part of All That is Good

In moments rare there comes to me

A vision unexpected;

I clearly see within my soul

The universe reflected.

I am a part of all that's good,

I feel, I know no limit;

For God in all stands forth so clear,

No fancied ills can dim it.

No matter what life's future hours

May hold of earthborn sadness,

I know there comes to me in truth

A heritage of gladness

That far transcends all grosser things

I've caught the vision glorious:

We all are a part of all that's good,

And good shall be victorious.

Anonymous Author

There are three ways that can be especially helpful in training our minds and hearts to see beyond everyday external events and into the realms of the numinous, where the Presence of God is:

- ❖ Distinguishing between thoughts and feelings. This takes practice. Often times, you will ask someone their opinion, and they will respond by telling you how they feel. Likewise, you will sometimes ask someone how they are feeling and find that they will instead share their opinion. This may be because in many people's minds, thoughts and feelings are jumbled together and seem like the same thing. When you can start to clearly differentiate between thoughts and feelings, and use thinking words deliberately and separately from feeling words, you will know you are beginning to evolve spiritually.

- ❖ Searching for patterns. Some people seem self absorbed in that they just get bored or frustrated if the conversation goes for too long without being about them. I used to be like this. I think it may be the result of growing up as an only child and thinking in I mode more often than others mode. Then there are those people who think of themselves as flexible, but would be surprised to discover that others experience them as rigid or aloof. What both groups of people have in common, ultimately, is a weakness in their ability to identify patterns within their own life. Now that I can look at events in my own life and identify reoccurring patterns in those events, I can identify both my responsibility as well as others' responsibilities for the impact they had on my life, in the manifestation of these pattern. As Johnny Nash's song says, "I can see clearly now the rain is gone, I can see all obstacles in my way, Gone are the dark clouds that had me blind, It's gonna be a bright, bright, sunshiny day!" This was the first time in many years that could see that I was beginning to mature spiritually in this previously undeveloped area.

❖ Imagining a life-review at the end of your life. It has often been said that people who do the work of personal growth often find themselves picturing in their mind a future moment at the end of their lifespan when their entire life will flash before their eyes. At that moment, they will be able to re-experience the positive and negative differences that they made in the world during their lifetime. They imagine they will be able to feel how they made other people feel. Actually, this is what I think of after my daily quiet prayer time and meditation on God's Word. I begin each day with a clear intention of having the greatest positive impact. I want to help other people to feel seen, heard and understood, so that compassion and service oriented lifestyle flows through me. It gives me great joy to help others selflessly. It is more about others, life was never all about me. In this area also, I realize my growth in evolving spiritually.

The human life is a rich experience, a unique journey along which we all make many mistakes, and gradually, hopefully, we discover who we truly are and our divine purpose. Each of us has a gift every day, an opportunity to make fresh choices that make a positive, rather than a negative, impact on others' lives. May each decision align with our divine purpose. No matter our past, each of us can choose to better reflect who you are meant to be, a fulfilment of God's plan for our lives. "For I know the plans I have for you," declares the Lord, *"plans to prosper you and not to harm you, plans to give you hope and a future. Then you will call upon me and come and pray to me, and I will listen to you. You will seek me and find me when you seek me with all of your heart. I will be found by you,"* declares the Lord. Jeremiah 29:11-14a, New International Version. As the following words motivate us:

Well the time has finally arrived. You can't run anymore. There is nowhere else you can hide. You've been searching oh so very long but right now give in while the feeling's strong. Choose ye today whom you will serve. Will it be God or man? Without a moment to loose, you must choose. –Marvin Winans

BE WISE WITH YOUR GREATEST POWER

From the day we are born until the day we die, we each will make numerous choices that affect not only our own lives, but others' lives as well. Sometimes, those choices are made without thinking and taking the proper steps to make the wisest choice. A choice is a decision, a green light to move forward, a yellow light to pause, or a red light to stop altogether. When we make the best choices, we align ourselves to live the happiest life possible, just as a global positioning device uses longitude and latitude to determine one's location as accurately as possible.

This human journey called life typically follows a timeline during which many people tend to make the major life decisions within approximately the same periods of time. Yet the true adventure is learning who we truly are within by venturing into learning to value ourselves, our priorities and our unique gifts. Growth is a process, one to enjoy, although we don't always appreciate the difficulties while we are experiencing them. However, this life we live is certainly a mystery, filled with challenges to learn and own our personal truths, to grow in wisdom and knowledge, be of service to others, and choose that which will be the healthiest and most beneficial to us.

In my experience, as a retired veteran bilingual teacher with 30 years of service, specializing in educational technology, I have humbly learned that I do not know everything. Therefore I am a continual learner, striving to grow wiser and apply what I have learned to be of service to others.

By navigating through life's many experiences, I have learned a vast amount of wisdom either directly from both my own choices or vicariously from the choices others have made.

In my opinion, there is not enough wisdom being shared to enlighten people, for we each have been given a gift, a power, to choose. Sadly, many people choose poorly, not realizing until later in life that they could have done things better. To illustrate this, I saw a cartoon in which a single woman was given three wishes by a genie that appeared after she rubbed a magic lamp. She wished for wealth, then beauty and paused before making her final wish. The genie asks, "What is your final wish?" "Ah," she tells the genie, "For my final wish, turn my cat Bob into a handsome, loving husband." Poof! Bob the cat suddenly became a man. He stood before her, an athletic, muscular, handsome Adonis. She smiled as he embraced her tenderly, whispering gently in her ear, "Makes you wish you hadn't had me neutered, doesn't it?"

Here is a clear example of a choice that may not have been considered to be of personal impact prior to the three wishes being granted. Since life is a series of choices, or decisions which determine our degree of happiness, let us delve into the types of life decisions that shape our lives and the realities we create for ourselves in our interactions with others. That said, here are the major life decisions that most people make during their lifetime.

Your health

How you think of yourself

Your values

Your attitude

Your life philosophy

Your aspirations

Your inspirations

How you handle life's many transitions

Your first job

How you handle relationships

Your choice to interact or remain aloof

How you handle issues at work

Your friends

How much money you save

How much you buy

Your education and/or continuing education

Your soulmate or spouse

How you raise your children

Your second career/changing jobs

Your retirement

Your level of involvement in community service

Something to consider

Vicki Evans

In the gardens of our lives

Where thoughts and ideas run wild

Weeds are ever trying to thrive

The slightest weakness lets them survive.

Be vigilant every day

As you go about your way

Guard what you hear, think and say

To live more Christlike in every way.

Choices that Impact the Quality of Daily Life

All of our choices make the difference, so choose wisely, for your greatest power is to choose. Many people think gardening is something you only do where there is dirt. However, realize that every day, we are tending our garden as planting seeds of ideas, mowing down weeds of unproductivity, tending our thought life which impacts our actions, leading others by example as a wise sage leads the novice gardener through useful tips and tricks of the trade to improve crops. In short, life is the garden and we are the gardeners whose choices make the difference between fertile harvests and dismal defeat. Herein lies the road we choose to travel. Choose wisely.

"Do not anticipate trouble, or worry about what may never happen. Keep in the sunlight." ~ Benjamin Franklin

Finally brethren, whatever is true, whatever is honorable, whatever is right, whatever is pure, whatever is lovely, whatever is of good repute, if there is any excellence and if anything worthy of praise, dwell on these things. Philippians 3:8

BE CAREFUL TO REFLECT AND REDIRECT

"May you live every day of your life."
—Jonathan Swift

A few days ago I watched a news broadcast show a grieving family mourning the sudden loss of their teenage daughter. There was intense mourning, reflecting on her accomplishments in school and the warm memories shared by friends and family. It made me wonder how often we each re-evaluate our purpose as we move forward in life's journey. In the aftermath of such a tragedy, our thinking is reframed, maybe even totally overhauled with regards to how we approach our lives, our goals, and our relationships.

As I watched the broadcast I suddenly realized how the fragility of life makes every moment more meaningful. Many of us waste far too many moments immersing ourselves in needless distractions that steal our attention away from the things and the people that really matter.

If you feel like you're on the wrong track with what matters most to you, here are nine warning signs to look for, and tips to get you back on track:

1. You need to make all of life's decisions on your own. You are in the driver's seat of your life.

Some people seem to live their entire lives on the default setting, much like the settings that come with your new computer or electronic device, never realizing that they can customize everything. Each of us has a unique passion in our heart for something that makes us feel alive. It's each person's duty to find it and keep that passion fire lit. You've got to stop caring so much about what everyone else wants you to do, and start actually living for yourself with God's guidance.

1. Find your talents, your unique gifts and abilities, your strength, your love, your passions and embrace them. God created each person to be a unique vessel of autonomy, free will and choice. Determine what your goals and focus are. You are empowered to choose, design and experience your life. The life you create from doing something that moves you is far better than the life you get from sitting around wishing you were doing it. So get up and get after it.

2. Make your life choices confidently based on facts, doing your own research and accepting sound advice.

Never let your fear decide your future. To play it too safe is one of the riskiest choices you can make. Accept what is, let go of what was and have faith in what could be. The bold steps you take into the unknown won't be easy, but every step is worth it. There's no telling how many miles you will have to run while chasing a dream, but this chase is what gives meaning to life. Even if you have to fail several times before you succeed, your worst attempt will always be 100% better than the person who settles and never tries at all.

3. Choose the best possible path, not the easiest possible path.

Nothing in life is easy. Don't expect things to be given to you. Go out and achieve them. Good things come to those who work for them. Some have natural talent, while others make up for it with tremendous heart and determination, and it's almost always the latter group that succeeds in the long run.

There is too much emphasis on finding a 'quick fix' in today's society. For example taking diet pills to lose weight instead of exercising and eating well. No amount of magic fairy dust replaces diligent, focused, hard work.

Working and training for something is the opposite of hoping for it. If you believe in it with all your heart, then work for it with all your might.

Great achievements must be earned. There is no elevator to success; you must take the stairs. So forget how you feel and <u>remember what you deserve</u>. NOW is always the best time to break out of your shell and show the world who you really are and what you're really made of. Start right where you are, use what you have, do what you can, and give it your best shot.

4. See the golden opportunities in the obstacles that you see.

The big difference between an obstacle and an opportunity is how you look at it. Look at the positives and don't dwell on the negatives. If you keep your head down, you'll miss life's goodness.

There's no shortage of problems waiting to be addressed. When you see problems piled on top of problems, and when there seems to be no end to the work that must be done in order to resolve them, what are you really seeing? You're looking at a mountain of opportunity. You're looking at a situation in which you can truly make a difference. You're looking at an environment where you can reach great heights by raising the stakes and pulling the reality of what's possible along with you.

When you look at an obstacle, but see opportunity instead, you become a powerful source that transforms grief into greatness.

5. Work smarter, not harder.

To achieve success and sustain happiness in life, you must focus your attention on the right things, in the right ways. Every growing human being (that means all of us) has resource constraints: limited time and energy. It is critical that you manage your resources effectively. You have to stay laser-focused on doing the RIGHT work, instead of doing a bunch of inconsequential work, right.

Not all work is created equal. Don't get caught up in odd jobs, even those that seem urgent, unless they are also important. Don't confuse being busy with being productive.

6. Finish the projects that you have started.

We are judged by what we finish, not what we start. Period.

Think about it, you rarely fail for the things you do. You fail for the things you don't do, the business you leave unfinished, and the things you make excuses about for the rest of your life.

In all walks of life, passion is what starts it and dedication is what finishes it.

7. Make time to connect with others in a meaningful way.

Never get so busy making a living that you forget to make a life for yourself. Never get so busy that you don't have time to be kind and connect with others. The happiest lives are connected to quality relationships. If you are too busy to share an occasional laugh with someone, you are too busy.

Truth be told, sometimes we're so busy watching out for what's just ahead of us that we don't take time to enjoy where we are and who we're with. So lift your head up today and appreciate those standing beside you. The people you take for granted today may turn out to be the only ones you need tomorrow.

Oh, and if you're currently on the fast track to success, be sure to be nice to people on your way up, because you might meet them again on your way back down. Remember life is a circle. Everything comes back around.

8. Concentrate your time on your support network because they make time for you.

Wrong things happen when you trust and worry about the wrong people. Don't make too much time for people who rarely make time for you, or who only make time for you when it's convenient for them. Know your worth. Know the difference between what you're getting from people and what you deserve.

Surround yourself with those who will support you whether it rains or shines. Above all, remember that people come and people go. That's life. Stop holding on to those who have let go of you long ago.

9. Make a positive difference in others' lives.

Needless drama doesn't just walk into your life out of nowhere; you either create it, invite it or associate with those who bring it. Do not let anyone's ignorance, hate, drama or negativity stop you from being the best person you can be.

Be an example of a pure existence. Don't spew hostile words at someone who spews them at you. Ignore their foolish antics and focus on kindness. Communicate and express yourself from a place of peace, from a place of love, with the best intentions. Use your voice for good: to inspire, to encourage, to educate, and to spread compassion and understanding.

If someone insists on foisting their hostility and drama on you, <u>simply ignore them and walk away</u>. Sometimes people will talk about you when they envy the life you lead. Let them be. You affected their life; don't let them affect yours. Those who create their own drama deserve their own karma. Don't get sidetracked by people who are not on track.

Keep looking ahead to prepare for the next steps.

If you are reading this, smile. Although nothing in life is ever guaranteed, you can always choose to make the present a positive, productive experience.

What you do with this moment is what's most important, because the present is the steering wheel of your life. The only difference between where you are and where you want to be, at any point in time, is what you are presently doing. Your present actions can instantly steer you onto the right track. From this moment forward everything changes if you want it to. You simply have to decide what to do right now.

Take time to reflect on your choices and their impact.

In what way have you traveled down the wrong track in life? What have you learned and what changes have you made?

THE BEST DAY EVER

I just woke up and I realized
It's the best day ever
Of my glorious life

First of all
I am alive
What a gift
Lord I give You a high five!

Didn't have to wake up
Coulda been dead
But God saw fit
To give me life instead

Got out of bed
Grateful and glad
That I'm moving my body
No pain, no feeling bad

Looked in the mirror
Look at me!
I am so thankful
That I can see!

LIVE SUNNY SIDE UP!

Opened my mouth
Said "Thank You Lord"
For the ability to even
Say a single word

Looked all around me
With a smile on my face
Just to have some food
And not be hungry in this place

Looked up above me
And began to cry
For this roof over my head
Not on the street to die

Looked in my pocket
How I rejoice
There's money in there
Help me make a wise choice

Tears are flowing
Oh my, I can hear
Clock ticking, birds singing
With my open, working ears

My heart is so happy

To love and be loved

As evidenced daily

By all these gifts from above

Peace and joy

Just happy to be

It's the best day ever

Full of opportunity!

Written by Vicki Evans

Copyright Marvic Music

Start each day with joy and unending gratitude. No matter how easy it is to grumble, to shuffle groggily and to moan in complaint, instead choose to use that same energy to smile, rejoice, laugh and be grateful!

As my poem says, think of all that you can give thanks to God for. A brand new day of life. Air to breathe, the ability to make a difference, people who care about you, and so much more if you just think about it. Make it a habit to count your blessings instead of counting your sorrows. You are here. Life is a gift. What to you do with gifts? Whine and speak negatively? Of course not! Rejoice, show gratitude. You have a purpose, and a chance to make a difference in others' lives. So, get after it. Fun, grateful, positive, productive and healthy thoughts are not merely for children, you know, nor only for the rich, nor only for the happy go lucky. You need fun, joy, purpose, love and laughter just as much as you need air and food!

Maybe you feel that each day seems alike, dull, gray and grim. Maybe you are irritated by the little things, as you drag yourself to do one task after another. Maybe you isolate yourself from people for a variety of reasons, maybe you are thinking about all the wrongs that have been done to you, choosing not to "be so bothered with people." Maybe as you look in your mailbox, you then wonder why the invitations stop coming. Maybe you really aren't really sick but you're far from feeling well. Well, whatever the maybes are in your life, choose to stop and retool your thinking. For all you know, things are not as grim as they seem. Just the other day, I was driving to work. Things looked so fuzzy but it was a clear day. I thought to myself, "You need to clean this front window." So I did, but things didn't look any better. I leaned over to get my lint free towel out of the door's side pocket. My prescription Transition eyeglasses fell off. I picked them up and just as I started to put them back on, I saw all the dust that had gathered on them overnight. After cleaning them, I laughed at myself, thinking "Now that's a shame. Look at the difference now that I've cleaned my glasses!" So don't be so quick to judge the world around you. It may just be your perspective needs to be cleared like my eyeglasses. For when you change, everything around you changes.

Here's another thing to consider. Maybe you are always tired. Think about your daily schedule. Maybe you are a workaholic as I used to be before I learned to manage my time more strategically to balance my work with leisure. It is not always hard work that drains off your energy, but emotional disengagement as well as emotional upheaval are both unrecognized energy vampires. With those constant unguarded thoughts and negatively entrenched habits, your happiness and peacefulness are much more likely to become troubled. Choose to refocus your thoughts. For as a man (or woman) thinks, so is he (or she).

Keep your heart free from hate. Keep your mind free from worry. Live simply, expect little but give much. Fill your life with love. Scatter sunshine. Forget about yourself and think more often of others.

Do as you would have done unto you. For every day above ground, in my opinion, is the best day ever. Why?

THE BEST DAY EVER: SEEING WITH NEW EYES

Today, when I awoke, I suddenly realized that this is the best day of my life, ever! There were times when I wondered if I would make it to today; but I did! And because I did I'm going to celebrate!

Today, I'm going to celebrate what an unbelievable life I have: all of the relationships, the accomplishments, the many blessings, the opportunities, and yes, even the hardships because they have served to make me stronger and wiser.

I will go through this day with my head held high, with a happy heart. I will marvel at God's many amazing gifts: the morning dew, the sun, the clouds, the trees, the flowers, that butterfly passing by, the cat sitting on a post, the joyful gait of a puppy walking with its owner and even the rejoicing, ever singing birds. Today, none of these miraculous creations will escape my notice.

Today, I will share my excitement for life with other people. I'll make someone smile. I'll go out of my way to perform an unexpected act of kindness for someone I don't even know.

Today, I'll give a sincere compliment to someone who seems down. I'll tell a child how special he is, and I'll tell someone I love just how deeply I care for them and how much they mean to me.

Today is the day I quit worrying about what I don't have and start being grateful for all the wonderful things God has already given me. I'll remember that to worry is just a waste of time because my faith in God and his Divine Plan ensures everything will be just fine. Tonight, before I go to bed, I'll go outside and raise my eyes to the heavens. I will stand in awe at the beauty of the stars and the moon, and I will praise God for these magnificent treasures.

As the day ends and I lay my head down on my pillow, I will thank Him for the best day of my life. I will sleep the sleep of a contented child, excited with expectation because I know that just as today was the best day ever, tomorrow will be too, because my loving Heavenly Father is working everything out for good for me, just as He promised in Romans 8:28, due to my abundant love for Him, since He has called me for His purpose. Therefore, every day is going to be the best day ever!

May we never forget that this life is a gift. The words from a song I heard on the way to work share the excitement for life we are to have: "Mr. Sun came out and he smiled at me. Said it's gonna be a good one just wait and see!" So let's choose to enjoy this wondrous journey called life and be grateful for this gift!

Every good and perfect gift is from above, coming down from the Father of the heavenly lights, who does not change like shifting shadows. James 1:17

Be led by the Holy Spirit. *Now the Lord is the Spirit, and where the Spirit of the Lord is, there is liberty(emancipation from bondage, freedom).* 2 Corinthians 3:17

Be free in Christ. *And I will walk at liberty and at ease, for I have sought and inquired for (and desperately required) Your precepts.* Psalm 119:45

Be uncomplicated. *I am the Door; anyone who enters in through Me will be saved (will live). He will come in and he will go out (freely), and will find pasture.* John 10:9

Be confident in God. *Lean on, trust in, and be confident in the Lord with all your heart and mind and do not rely on your own insight or understanding.* Proverbs 3:5

Be quick to forgive. *Bear with each other and forgive whatever grievances you may have against one another. Forgive as the Lord forgave you.* Colossians 3:13

Be outrageously blessed. *Delight yourself also in the Lord, and He will give you the desires and secret petitions of your heart.* Psalm 37:4

Through it all, may this book inspire you to live more joyfully, enjoy life and thrive by living a grateful life.

Epilogue

Let Your Spirit Be Positive

Be joyful always; pray continually; give thanks in all circumstances, for this is God's will for you in Christ Jesus. — I Thessalonians 5:16-18

By nature, some of us tend to be sour, negative people, who see and comment on the bad things in life. Then there are those who appear overly optimistic, seeing the positive where there is absolutely nothing positive. That type of person needs to be realistic. On the other hand, there are those of us who tend to be positive, offering kindness, a good word or encouragement at the appropriate time.

I Thessalonians 5:16-18 show us that every Christian is designed to live a joyful, prayerful and thankful life at all times. Having a joy-filled, cheerful heart is excellent medicine for us in addition to causing us to be a blessing to others, according to Proverbs 17:22, which says, *"A cheerful heart is good medicine..."* Through consistent prayer we are attuned to the Lord's purposes as He enables us to wait expectantly for His divine intervention.

Having an attitude of gratitude continuously, no matter what happens, keeps our attention on our Almighty God, Who loves us limitlessly and is always faithful. It pleases Him when we have a lifestyle that inspires others and if fulfilling for us.

Finally, brothers, whatever is true, whatever is right, whatever is pure, whatever is lovely, whatever is admirable, if anything is excellent or praiseworthy, think about such things. Herein Philippians 2:8 encourages us to have a positive attitude by thinking about that which is admirable, noble, true or excellent. Since we live in an era that is

204

conducive to doing wrong, let us be discerning and exercise wisdom in offering our respect and positive acceptance of those in authority.

*Obey your leaders and submit to their authority. They keep watch over you as men who must give and account. Obey them so that their work will be a joy, not a burden, for that would be of no advantage to you. –*Hebrews 13:17

Let us be also be forgiving encouragers of each other, acting and reacting with the mind of Christ.

*Do not be overcome by evil, but overcome evil with good. –*Romans 12:21

*Bear with each other and forgive whatever grievances you may have against one another. Forgive as the Lord forgave you. And over all these virtues put on love, which binds them all together in perfect unity. Let the peace of Christ rule in your hearts, since as members of one body you were called to peace. And be thankful. Let the Word of Christ dwell in you richly. –*Colossians 3:13-16

It is vital to have a positive attitude toward our circumstances, for it is easy to be joyful and grateful when all is well. Yet we need to realize that it is not our circumstances that make us unhappy; actually, it is our negative attitude. Let us remember that suffering is inevitable, but misery is a choice.

With Christ, the Hope of Glory, walking beside us, living within us, praying for us, and holding our hands as we traverse through life's journey, we are inseparable from His love and intertwined intimately with Him. What an amazing, glorious wonder that surpasses all we can understand! When we quietly spend time communing and worshipping prayerfully in His presence, our awareness of His Life within us is heightened.

Such knowledge is humbling and awesome beyond compare, producing within us the Joy of the Lord, which is our Strength. He fills us with Peace and Joy so that we may bubble over by the power of the Holy Spirit. Surely, through Him, our cup overflows. Remember:

More *Jesus*
Less Drama
Less Selfishness
Less Complaining
Less Bitterness
Less Gossip
Less Pride
Less Anger
Less Me

To them God has chosen to make known among the Gentiles the glorious riches of this mystery, which is Christ in you, the Hope of Glory. Colossians 1:27

Nehemiah said, "Go and enjoy choice food and sweet drinks, and send some to those who have nothing prepared. This day is sacred to our Lord. Do not grieve, for the Joy of the Lord is your strength. – Nehemiah 8:10

Remember also that we are called to trust in God. Sure, life often deals us an evil blow, yet we must remember that God is the One Who can turn this bad into good in the end. So cancel all pity parties, give God thanks and look expectantly towards the good solution He will bring about. This demonstrates our maturity as we trust in God, remain appreciative and stay positive, for He gives us strength. Be encouraged, be joyful and keep the faith, remembering the words of Philippians 4:12-13:

I know what it is to be in need, and I know what it is to have plenty. I have learned the secret of being content in any and every situation, whether well fed or hungry, whether living in plenty or in want. I can do everything through Him Who gives me strength. - Philippians 4:12-13

In closing, may the following bless, strengthen and uplift you, enabling to do greater things to God's glory, as He has purposed you to do. Live joyfully!

May the God of your hope so fill you with all joy and peace in believing [through the experience of your faith] that by the power of the Holy Spirit, you may abound and be overflowing (bubbling over) with hope. – Romans 15:13 Amplified Bible

The Lord bless thee, and keep thee: The Lord make His face shine upon thee, and be gracious unto thee: The Lord lift up His countenance upon thee, and give thee peace. –Numbers 6:24-26

JESUS FIRST
OTHERS SECOND
YOURSELF LAST

Let the Light guide you, let wisdom inspire you and let love enable you to grow, know and glow.

About the Author

Aurora A. Ambrose is a retired bilingual educator who has taught students of all ages for three decades and trained new teachers for 12 years. Aurora's love for philanthropy, the arts, prose, lyrics, and poetry has inspired her to motivate and encourage others, just as she has chosen to do throughout her life. Ambrose's writing experience includes, but is not limited to:

Poetry Collections

Children's Books

Annual Journals for the non-profit, Los Angeles Music Week

Songwriting, registered with BMI, Broadcast Music International:

- ❖ As Soon As the Weather Breaks Bobby Blue Bland

- ❖ Another Blues DayMargie Evans

- ❖ Mistreated WomanMargie Evans

- ❖ Can't Get You Off My MindMargie Evans

Album Liner Notes

- ❖ Too Late Rising Sun

- ❖ Another Blues Day

- ❖ We Shall Walk Through the Valley in Peace

Ambrose's faith and interests provide her with opportunities to give service in ways that benefit the community. A continual learner and avid reader, she studies to stay current on technology as well as varied methods of professional and personal growth. With a passion to help others, Aurora has a full and grateful heart, and desires to enrich others' lives by helping them see the silver lining of opportunity and purpose that are ever present in each one of life's many faith producing dark clouds.

www.ingramcontent.com/pod-product-compliance
Lightning Source LLC
Chambersburg PA
CBHW061201040426
42445CB00023B/716